KEZIAH @ 50 :

THE JOURNEY CALLED LIFE

KEZIAH TWUMASI

KEZIAH @ 50 –THE JOURNEY CALLED LIFE

Copyright © June 2024 by Keziah Twumasi

Keziah Twumasi

theladykeziah@gmail.com

+233 (0) 244 043911

ISBN 978 – 9988 – 3 – 8250 – 6

Keziah @ 50 – The Journey Called Life is a registered trademark of the **Zizikarl Foundation.**

CONTENTS

DEDICATION

To my Golden Jubilee

(50th Birthday - Saturday, 14th September 2024)

The capacity to march on regardless not as a novice but as a woman with great experience, awesome community and clarity of purpose.

To God be the glory.

ACKNOWLEDGEMENTS

To Rev. Karlton, Ziah and Martin Luther. To everyone who contributed to my life in whichever way; pain, pleasure or purpose, you have helped in shaping me into the woman I am becoming. I can never love who I am without loving the journey that took me here. Thank you all. As in the words of Andrea Dykstra "*In order to love who you are, you cannot hate the experiences that shaped you.*" I truly love the woman I am becoming.

I was blessed to have the assistance and support of many gifted and talented people to whom I want to express my sincere appreciation. You know that feeling when those you call "*yours*" neglect and abandon you and the universe sends serendipities your way.

To you, Avila Masvaya, may your soul rest in perfect peace. You are gone but not forgotten. I envy the angels in heaven.

I am grateful

INTRODUCTION

Keziah @ 50: The Journey Called Life

Life is often likened to a journey, a winding path that leads us through valleys of challenges and peaks of triumphs. Each step, each turn, carries with it a story - an intricate tapestry woven from moments of joy, sorrow, learning and growth. This book, *"Keziah @ 50: The Journey Called Life"* is a celebration of one such remarkable journey, the life of Keziah, a woman whose fifty years have been a testament to resilience, love and the indomitable human spirit.

Keziah's story, which she has put into epistles is not just her own; it is a narrative that resonates with universal themes of perseverance, transformation and self-discovery. Born into a world filled with expectations and limitations, Keziah carved her own path, defying odds and breaking barriers. Her journey is a vivid illustration of how one can navigate life's unpredictable currents with dedication and determination.

From the innocence of childhood to the complexities of adulthood, from the pursuit of dreams to the reality of setbacks, Keziah's life encapsulates the essence of what it means to be human. It is a chronicle of experiences that have shaped her into the person she is today - a woman of strength, wisdom and unwavering faith. Her fifty years are a mosaic of memories, each piece contributing to the beautiful portrait of her existence.

As you turn the pages of this book, you will travel through time, witnessing the evolution of a life lived fully and passionately, which she has penned down as epistles. You will experience the moments that defined her and uncover the lessons that guided her. This is an exploration of the human condition through the eyes of someone who has embraced life's journey with open arms and an open heart.

Keziah @ 50: The Journey Called Life invites you to reflect on your own journey, to find inspiration in Keziah's letters and to appreciate the myriad ways in which life unfolds. It is a reminder that every journey, no matter how ordinary or extraordinary, holds the power to teach, transform and inspire.

Welcome to Keziah's world. Let her journey illuminate yours.

PREFACE

The little daughter of Mr. Geoffrey Christian Awuku-Budu of blessed memory and Madam Lucy Parry is fifty years today, hurray!

Keziah Akosua Takyiwah Awuku-Budu was my maiden name. I grew up in a polygynous ambient, where every wife had to fight for a piece of the cake for her children.

I could not help being not just nostalgic but wistful with writing this book. I would have loved to have photos of my childhood, my toddling moments, memories of my childhood with either parents, siblings, niblings or piblings – but nothing. How I wish to have had photos of my childhood when I started the Experimental Preparatory School in Nsawam in the Eastern Region of Ghana for my basic school education - but nothing. Attending a preparatory school then was regarded as an upgrade. I am grateful to my parents. However, what mattered to me the most was the constellation of moments I yearned to have had at that tender age. In 1983, in the midst of famine in Ghana, my father had so much and could feed many others.

I sat for the common entrance examination and passed so I had to continue to a secondary school. My father gave the assurance that he had visited my first-choice school so we were waiting for prospectus to organise my necessities for school, which turned out to be a hoax. Nine days to school reopening, my mother looked at me and said, *"You have not even developed breast buds yet, you will be twelve on your next birthday, if you could sit for common entrance and pass, you will attend a secondary school."* Lo and behold, she secured admission, got my prospectus and I was ready by the reopening date to start my secondary school education at Benkum Secondary School, Larteh Akuapem in the Eastern Region. How could a father who provided for many others forget his very own? Today, I have beautiful personal ties with some old students of my alma mater. When we replace *why is this happening to me* with what is this trying to teach me, - everything shifts.

Through my university education from Jayee University to the University of Ghana - Legon, even when I had married, everything indicated that I am the architect of my own fate. There has been the good, the bad and the ugly moments but what I am super excited about is the future because that little, naïve and ignorant girl has metamorphosed into an adult who is in control of her beliefs, paradigms and perspectives; ready, willing and able to live, move and have her being as ordained. With a positive mindset and right perspective to life, anyone can form his or her own family at any given time. A family devoid of sibling rivalry, unhealthy competition, counterproductive comparisons and entitlement.

I encourage you to turn your wounds into wisdom and your pain into power. In addition, use your mistakes as stepping-stone to higher heights. Everything is possible to the soul that is ready.

PROFILE

Her mission is assisting people to reconnect with themselves, own their lives and live their dreams as ordained. She is a global speaker, author, entrepreneur and coach.

She is a licensed Psychosocial Counsellor with over two decades of experience in working with people; providing a skilled professional counselling to individuals, family and group for the purpose of improving their well-being, alleviating distress and enhancing coping skills.

Keziah Twumasi is a remarkable woman who wears many hats. She is an accomplished author, a captivating speaker, successful entrepreneur, compassionate coach and humanitarian leader.

She is the author of *"Getting Married and Staying Married,"* a book that has inspirited and touched the lives of many. Her words have the power to uplift, motivate and transform individuals, leaving a lasting impact on their journey towards personal growth and self-discovery. Through her writing, she shares her own experiences, wisdom and insights, guiding readers towards a path of fulfilment and purpose.

In addition to her writing, Lady Keziah is a sought-after keynote speaker who captivates audiences with her powerful presence and eloquent delivery.

Her speeches are not only informative but also deeply inspiring, leaving listeners with a renewed sense of hope and determination.

She has the ability to connect with people from all walks of life, encouraging them to overcome challenges and pursue their dreams relentlessly.

Lady Keziah's entrepreneurial spirit is evident in her various successful ventures. She is the founder and executive director of the Zizikarl Foundation and the CEO of TheLadyKeziah's Consult, each one a testament to her dedication and drive. Her ability to identify opportunities and turn them into profitable ventures has earned her respect and admiration in the business world. Her entrepreneurial journey serves as an inspiration to aspiring business owners, proving that with passion and hard work, anyone can achieve great success.

As a coach, Lady Keziah is known for her empathy, understanding and ability to guide individuals towards their goals. She has a unique talent for helping others tap into their full potential, providing them with the tools and support they need to overcome obstacles and achieve personal and professional success. Her coaching style is nurturing yet challenging, pushing individuals out of their comfort zones and helping them unlock their true potential.

Despite her many roles and accomplishments, Lady Keziah remains humble and grounded. She is a woman of faith and her spirituality shines through in everything she does. Her unwavering belief in the power of God and the importance of living a purpose-driven life is evident in her work, her relationships and her interactions with others.

In conclusion, Lady Keziah is a remarkable woman who has dedicated her life to making a positive impact on others. Through her writing, speaking engagements, humanitarian services, entrepreneurial ventures and coaching, she has touched the lives of countless individuals, inspiring them to live their best lives. Her commitment to personal growth, her entrepreneurial spirit and her unwavering faith makes her a true force to reckon with.

Credit

Osagyefo Kwaku Aboagye

Asuogyaman Ambassador

CHAPTER ONE

Behind the Mask

Hiding the hurt, hiding the pain

Hiding the tears that fall like rain.

Saying I am fine, when I am anything but.

This ache in my soul rips at my gut.

My skin is on fire, I burn from within

The calm on my face is an ongoing sin.

The world must stay out; I have built up a wall

My fragile lie will collapse should it ever fall.

Loneliness consumes me; it eats away the years

Until my life is swallowed by unending fears.

Waiting for someone to see I wear a mask

And care enough to remove it, is that too much to ask?

A Poem by Melisa Bernards

LETTERS TO MY YOUNGER SELF

Dear Akosua Takyiwah, the Younger Me,

As I sit down to write this letter, I want you to know that you are not alone. You may feel lost, confused, hurt, neglected and abandoned right now, but there is hope, and there is a brighter future waiting for you. I know because I have walked the path you are on and I have learned from the mistakes I have made. As a teenager, a young adult or younger woman, you are at a point you feel you need more out of life, you need to harness your passion, talents and gifts but there is no guide and a sense of direction. Many people are directing you to their journey but you really want your own path in this life, not to walk in the paths of anyone's. I understand the feeling very well and that is why I am writing this letter to you. Someday, everything with make perfect sense, so for now, laugh at the confusion, smile through the tears and keep reminding yourself that everything will work out together for your good.

Primarily, I want you to understand that the men in your life or the love you receive from others do not define your worth. You are enough just as you are. You are full of love and a genuine heart therefore understand that you deserve all the best that this universe has to offer you just as you are. You deserve to be treated with respect, kindness and love. Do not settle for anything less. Your journey may have been marked by loneliness and isolation but it is never too late to cultivate meaningful connections and friendships. Seek out communities that align with your interests and values and do not hesitate to reach out and connect with others.

Vulnerability can be terrifying but it is also the gateway to genuine connection and belonging.

I know it is arduous to imagine these right now but one day you will break free from the cycle of toxic relationships. You will learn how to love yourself, set boundaries and prioritize your own well-being above all else. Trust me when I say that walking away from those who do not value you will be the best decision you ever make. Learn now that before you chase anything in this world, you will have to be your own peace and joy.

Financial struggles may weigh heavily on your mind but remember that money does not define your worth either. Focus on building a future for yourself based on passion, purpose and perseverance. Work hard, work smart, pursue your dreams and never be afraid to ask for help when you need it. Look for opportunities that are beyond your skillset, good things happen when you challenge yourself. Build resilience and mental fortitude that will enable you to develop success from failures. Let every failure be your stepping-stone to higher levels. Do not give your time, energy and devotion to anything that does not bring you peace, profits or purpose. Financial struggles can feel overwhelming but they do not define your future. Learn to manage your finances wisely and seek opportunities for growth and stability. Remember that wealth comes in many forms, including the richness of experiences, friendships and personal growth.

Financial stability may seem like an elusive dream but with diligence, determination and wise choices, it is attainable. Educate yourself about money management, invest in your skills and education and do not be afraid to take calculated risks to pursue your goals. Remember that your worth is not tied to your bank accounts, although financial freedom can provide opportunities for growth and security. Understand that your happiness is not related to money. Money is to make you comfortable but that cannot be your source of happiness and joy.

For family, either nuclear or extended, I know the pain of feeling unloved and unsupported but please know that family is not just by consanguinity or affinity. Family is about whoever that is willing, ready and able to hold your hands when you need it the most. At a point in your life, you can create, form or design your own family. You can build community around any need in your life if you have the right mindset. Know that your beliefs, paradigms and perspectives to life will determine how you see the world, how you interpret the world and how you relate with people. You can create your own world regardless of what happens within your family. Seek out those who lift you up, those who believe in you and who stand by you through thick and thin and fully invest into those relationships. Learn how to compartmentalise your life by surrounding yourself with people who bring out the best in you and let go of those who bring you down. In your era, the world is a global village; you do not have to be a recluse. There is a huge difference between being alone and being lonely, do you get it?

Even in the midst of loneliness, remember that solitude can be a gift. Use that time to rediscover yourself, explore your interests and cultivate a deep sense of self-awareness and self-love. Embrace your uniqueness, cherish your independence and know that you are never truly alone. Those you call yours can neglect and abandon you, you can still become whomever you want to and build your own family. Many a time, the family you create can bring you more value than the family you come from. You have no reason to turn into a recluse and blame anyone for your inefficiencies in life. At a certain age, no one is responsible for how you turn out, YOU are responsible for YOURSELF. Take control of your life and do not live in the victim stage where you blame others for your poor choices and decisions. Surround yourself with people that push you to be better – higher goals, good vibes and positive energy.

As you embark on your unique journey in life, know that every experience, both good and bad, will shape you into the strong and resilient human you are destined to become. Believe in yourself, trust your instincts and never stop fighting for the life you deserve. Do not stop doing, trying, learning and experimenting until the miracle happens. Even in your mistakes, there are learning curves for you so do not be afraid to live your authentic self. Originals cost more than imitations, live genuinely and authentically and be unapologetic for it.

As you stand on the brink of owning your life, I want to offer you some guidance and encouragement, drawing from the lessons I have learned over the years. Your journey may have been rocky thus far but there is still so much ahead of you, waiting to be explored and experienced.

When it comes to love and relationships, choose a partner who uplifts and supports you, a partner who cherishes your presence and encourages your growth. Pay attention to red flags and do not ignore your intuition when it warns you of potential harm. Remember that love should never hurt, diminish or compromise your dignity. Do not accept struggle love, the woman who goes through series of hardships in her relationship is not precisely the good woman as society and religion speculate. *Oh, she is a good woman, upon all her man did; after everything her man put her through, she is still with him - that is a load of pretentious bollocks.* If a man loves and respects you as his partner, he will not take you through disdaining moments expecting you to normalise them. You are not a rehabilitating centre for badly raised people. It is not your job to fix any man, parent or raise him. You need a partner not a project as in the words of Julia Roberts. Do not marry the packaging, study the character; there are too many expired products in well-packaged containers. Break ups hurt but losing someone who does not respect and appreciate you is a gain not a loss.

As I sit down to write this letter, I can't help but feel a surge of emotions knowing what you are about to embark on. Turning 50 is a milestone, a moment of reflection and I want to share some wisdom I have gathered along the way, hoping you can extrapolate some principles, wisdom and knowledge to pre-empt and prevent you from going through unnecessary stress, ease the burdens you carry and guide you towards a brighter path.

As you navigate the vicissitudes of life, remember to be kind to yourself. You are human, flawed and imperfect but deserving of love and compassion nonetheless. Practice self-compassion, forgive yourself when you make mistakes and embrace the journey of self-discovery and personal growth with an open heart and mind. Life is like a roller coaster, it has its difficulties but you can choose to scream or enjoy the ride.

As I celebrate my 50th birthday, I want to take a moment to reflect on the lessons I have learned and the wisdom I gained along the way. If I could offer you one piece of advice as a teenager, a younger person under 50, it would be this: prioritize your purpose and well-being above all else. Define what self-actualisation means to you and work towards it. If you happen to get someone who loves you deeply, willing and able to build a life with you, invest all you have into the relationship and build each other up. When your path crosses with someone who not only believes in your potential but also actively contributes to your growth journey, know my darling that you have struck gold.

Life then becomes a shared adventure, where you both evolve side-by-side, inspiring and challenging each other to reach higher levels of greatness and authenticity.

Do not ever forget that growth is hard and change can be painful but there is nothing as painful as being stuck somewhere you do not belong. Do you understand? Do not settle for the crumbs when you deserve the whole cake.

Take note of the following also:

Firstly, one of the most important lessons I have learned is the power of boundaries. Learn to assert your needs, set boundaries with others and prioritize your well-being above all else. Surround yourself with people who respect and honour your boundaries and do not be afraid to walk away from those who do not. I urge you to prioritize self-care and self-discovery. Invest time in activities that bring you joy and fulfilment, whether it is pursuing your passions, exploring new hobbies or simply taking time to rest, relax and recharge. Your mental, emotional and physical well-being are invaluable assets that deserve your attention and nurturing.

Secondly, listen to your inner voice, trust your instincts and never ignore the red flags in any relationship. Ignoring red flags because you want to see the good in people will cost you dearly later. Know what your red flags are, what your deal breakers are and what are your non-negotiables in this life if not; people will only take you for granted.

The other side of the same coin is also so you do not lose valuable relationships because of your insecurities, traumas and trust issues that you need to heal. Until you have identified the monsters in yourself and slayed them, you will always try to find them in others. Nevertheless, understand that some people will only love you as much as they can use you. Their loyalty ends where their benefits end, mark them and avoid them. It is equally possible that you will know all the flaws of someone, their weaknesses and mistakes and still find them completely amazing. Nevertheless, do not forget that you cannot fix someone who does not want to be fixed; you will rather ruin your life trying.

Do not fall in love with a person's potential and neglect his reality. It is the reality you will live with; the potential might just be in your mind – your dream for the person, it might never materialise. You deserve to be with a man who respects, values, and treats you with kindness and compassion. Do not settle for less just because you are afraid of being alone. As in the words of Robin Williams, *"I used to think the worse thing in life was to end up all alone. It is not. The worst thing in life is to end up with people that make you feel all alone."* Respect yourself enough to say *"I deserve better."* Learn how to set boundaries, everyone will love you when you let them take you for granted, it is when you set boundaries and start checking things that you will know those who actually have your best interests at heart. Know your place in people's lives and live accordingly. It is not pride; it is called self-respect. Do not force for true love and true friends – these come to you naturally.

Choose YOU in all situations. What is meant for you will always feel natural, calm and clear, not forced, chaotic or confusing.

Thirdly, invest in yourself - physically, emotionally and intellectually. Take good care of your body, nurture your mind and pursue your passions with unbridled enthusiasm. Take good care of your mental health. When you start taking care of yourself, you start feeling better, you start looking better and you attract better. Everything begins with you. Do not be afraid to dream big, chase after your goals with relentless determination. Surround yourself with positive influences and seek out mentors who inspire you to be the best version of yourself. Learn from those who have walked the path before you and do not be afraid to ask for help when you need it. Remember, asking for help is a sign of strength not weakness. Take risks, embrace change and never let fear hold you back from pursuing your dreams. Life is too short to play it safe, so dare to step outside of your comfort zone and explore all that the world has to offer. In the words of Myles Munroe, *"The greatest tragedy in life is not death, but a life without purpose."*

Fourthly, family may have been absent or disappointing in your life but that does not diminish your worth or the love you are capable of giving and receiving. Seek out connections with those who uplift and support you, whether they are blood relatives or kindred spirits you meet along the way. Cultivate relationships that nourish your soul and remind you of your inherent goodness.

Lastly, embrace your individuality and authenticity wholeheartedly. Do not dim your light or hide your true self to please others. Your uniqueness is your greatest strength and the world needs your voice, your perspective and your contributions. Be unapologetically yourself and trust that those who are meant to be in your life will embrace you for who you are. Do not live to impress people, your journey is very different from everyone else's. Do not sacrifice your peace of mind for materials things to impress people who can turn their backs on you within a twinkle of an eye. Live your full life and potential not to prove any point to anyone but to live, move and have your being as ordained.

There will be bumps in the road, moments of doubt and unexpected detours but remember that every experience, good or bad, is an opportunity for growth and resilience. Keep moving forward with courage, compassion and an unwavering belief in yourself. You are capable of creating a life filled with love, abundance and fulfilment. You are the architect of your fate.

Above all else, never forget that you are worthy of love, happiness and fulfilment. Believe in yourself, love yourself and know that you are enough just as you are. The journey ahead may be challenging at times but I promise you, it will be worth it in the end. Never lose sight of your worth and potential. You are capable of far more than you realize and the world is brimming with opportunities waiting for you to seize them. Trust in yourself, believe in your abilities and never let anyone dim the light that shines within you.

May nothing eclipse your stardom in this journey.

With love and hope for the future.

Your Older Self,

Keziah

Dear Akosua Takyiwah, the Younger Me,

FAITH, RELIGION AND SPIRITUALITY

As you journey through life, grappling with questions of faith, religion and spirituality, I want to offer you some guidance from the perspective of my own experiences and reflections. While I cannot claim to have all the answers, I hope these words will help illuminate your path as you seek to connect with the divine in your own unique way.

First and foremost, I want you to know that your spiritual journey is deeply personal and sacred. It is not about conforming to external expectations or adhering to rigid doctrines; rather, it is about seeking truth, meaning and connection in a way that resonates with your heart and soul.

You may have been raised in a religious environment that emphasized the importance of attending gatherings and following prescribed rituals as a means of communing with God. While these practices can offer valuable opportunities for community support and shared worship, they are not the only pathways to divine connection.

True communion with the divine begins within you. God, the universe, the divine presence, the infinite power - however you choose to conceptualize it is not confined to the walls of a church, mosque, temple, or synagogue. He is omnipresent, dwelling within you and all around you, waiting to be discovered and embraced.

Take time to quiet your mind, open your heart and listen to the whispers of your soul. Engage in practices that nurture your spiritual growth and deepen your connection with the divine, whether it is through prayer, meditation, contemplation or simply spending time in nature. Seek out wisdom from diverse sources - spiritual texts, teachings - and discern what resonates with your innermost being.

Remember that spirituality is a journey of exploration, discovery and evolution. Allow yourself the freedom to question, doubt and explore different paths and perspectives along the way. Embrace the uncertainty and ambiguity, knowing that it is often in the depths of doubt and darkness that we discover the light of truth and illumination. Understand that there is a huge difference between religious activities and a relationship with God. The fact that you are seriously involved in a religious activity, regular and punctual does not mean you are connected deeply with God. People might praise you for your service but God looks beyond that.

Above all, trust your intuition and inner guidance. God speaks to each of us in the language of the heart, gently nudging us towards greater love, compassion and understanding.

Cultivate a relationship with the divine that is authentic, intimate, grounded in love and let your faith be a source of strength, inspiration and guidance as you navigate the highs and lows of life's journey.

May you walk your path with courage, grace and an unwavering faith in the divine presence that resides within you and all of creation.

With Love and Blessings.

Your Older Self,

Keziah

EMBRACING YOUR UNIQUE PATH

Dear Younger Me,

As I write this letter to you, I am filled with a deep sense of empathy and understanding for the journey you are about to embark on - a journey of self-discovery, authenticity and the courage to defy societal and religious expectations in pursuit of your own truth. In the pages that follow, I hope to offer you guidance and reassurance as you navigate the waters of conformity that is sometimes treacherous and carve out a path that is uniquely yours.

I want you to know that it is okay to be different, to defy the expectations placed upon you by society and religion and to forge your own path in life. You are not meant to live in the shadows of others or to conform to someone else's idea of who you should be. Your journey is yours alone and it is up to you to chart the course that feels most authentic and aligns with your deepest desires and values.

Society may try to pressure you into fitting into a narrow mould of acceptability - telling you how to dress, how to act, who to love and what to believe. Religion too may impose rigid opinions, doctrines and dogmas that leave little room for individual expression and exploration. Regardless, I urge you not to succumb to these external pressures, not to sacrifice your authenticity on the altar of conformity.

Instead, embrace your uniqueness, your quirks, your passions and your dreams. Celebrate the qualities that make you different from everyone else, for those are the very essence of who you are. Trust in your intuition and inner guidance and have the courage to follow the path that calls to you, even if it diverges from the well-worn roads of convention. Be careful of people pleasing, whatever you do, make sure it is the right thing to do and it is within your capacity to do it. Do not do anything or live any other way because of who is watching. There is a supreme being who can see beyond what humans can celebrate you for.

Self-discovery is a journey of exploration and growth - a journey that requires you to question, doubt and challenge the status quo. It is a journey of uncovering your deepest truths, your most cherished values and your highest aspirations - a journey that can only be undertaken with an open heart and a fearless spirit.

Do not be afraid to question the beliefs and traditions that are handed down to you. There is nothing wrong to seek out alternative perspectives and to forge your own understanding of the world and your place in it. Your truth may not look like everyone else's and that is perfectly okay. What matters most is that you live authentically in alignment with your own values and convictions.

As in the words of Eric Worre - the most successful network marketer and sought after coach and mentor, best-selling author and entrepreneur, **"Choose your hard, you can go through life with the regret of dealing with life at a fraction of your potential or you can have the satisfaction of building something that you actually deserve."** Therefore stay dedicated, if you are busy working on your goals and dreams, you are not missing out on anything.

As you navigate the complexities of life, remember that you are not alone. Surround yourself with people who accept you for who you are, support you on your journey of self-discovery and celebrate your uniqueness. Seek out communities and mentors who share your values and inspire you to be the best version of yourself. Do not follow mentors who are tormentors, you cannot live your truest authenticity with such people. Do not shrink yourself to fit places and people you outgrow.

Above all, trust in yourself and in the wisdom of your own inner voice. You have everything you need within you to navigate life's challenges and to create a life that is meaningful, fulfilling and true to who you are. Embrace your journey with courage, curiosity and an unwavering belief in the beauty of your own uniqueness.

With Love and Solidarity.

Your Older Self,

Keziah

Dear Akosua Takyiwah, the Younger Me,

YOUR BODY IS A TEMPLE, A SACRED VESSEL DESERVING OF REVERENCE AND RESPECT

As I reflect on the journey that has led me to this moment, there are truths I wish to impart to you - wisdom born of both joy and pain, lessons learned through the sometimes, harsh realities of love and relationships. I write to you now with the hope that my words may serve as a guiding light, illuminating the path ahead as you navigate the complexities of intimacy, desire and the longing for connection.

First and foremost, I want you to know that your worth is not measured by the attention or affection of men. You are whole and complete unto yourself, deserving of love, respect and tenderness. Never allow anyone to diminish your value or exploit your vulnerability for his or her own gratification.

In matters of the heart, it is crucial to distinguish between love and lust - to recognize the difference between fleeting passion and enduring devotion. Lust may be intense, all-consuming and seductive but it is often rooted in desire rather than genuine emotional connection. A man may shower you with affection, whisper sweet words of adoration and sponsor your lavish lifestyle. He may even marry you and share your bed night after night but that does not guarantee his heart is yours.

Love can mean different things to different people at different phases of their lives – you will have to generate or regenerate your definition at every given phase of your life.

True love transcends physical desire - it is patient, kind and unwavering in its commitment. It sees beyond the surface to the essence of who you are, cherishing your flaws as well as your virtues. It honours your autonomy, respects your boundaries and seeks your happiness above all else.

You may encounter men who claim to love you, yet their actions, which are directly opposite of their words – speak louder. Pay attention to how they treat you, how they make you feel and whether their intentions align with your definition. When their words conflict with their actions, believe their actions. How they treat you is how they feel about you. Trust your intuition, your gut instincts - they are your most reliable guides in matters of the heart.

Your body is a temple, a sacred vessel deserving of reverence and respect. Do not give yourself away lightly, succumbing to the whims of momentary desire or societal pressure. Your purity is not defined by your sexual experiences but by the integrity with which you honour yourself and your values.

Sexuality is a powerful force, a source of pleasure, intimacy and connection. Nonetheless, it is also a deeply personal choice, one that should be made with clarity, intention and mutual consent.

Do not allow anyone to coerce or manipulate you into compromising your boundaries or sacrificing your autonomy.

When the time comes to share yourself with a man, let it be a choice born of love, desire and genuine connection - not out of obligation or a misguided sense of duty. Honour your body, honour your heart and trust that the right man will cherish and respect you for who you are.

Above all, remember that you are worthy of a love that sees you, accepts you, and celebrates you in all your beauty and imperfection. Hold out for the kind of love that sets your soul on fire, that makes you feel seen, heard and valued beyond measure.

With Love and Solidarity.

Your Older Self,

Keziah

Dear Akosua Takyiwah, my Younger Self,

IT IS EASY TO STAND WITH THE CROWD, IT TAKES COURAGE TO STAND ALONE

As I write this letter to you, I am filled with a sense of both nostalgia and urgency, knowing the journey you are about to embark on and the challenges you will face along the way. In a world that often seems to prioritize superficiality over substance and conformity over authenticity, I want to offer you guidance on how to navigate with integrity and staying true to yourself no matter the pressures of society.

Living in integrity means aligning your actions, beliefs and values with your true self even when it is difficult or unpopular to do so. It means being honest with yourself and others, standing up for what you believe in and refusing to compromise your principles for the sake of acceptance or approval. In a society that may seek to degrade your sense of self-worth, it is essential to cultivate a strong sense of self-awareness and self-respect. Know your own worth, recognize your inherent dignity and value as a human being and refuse to let anyone diminish or undermine your sense of worthiness.

Be mindful of the company you keep and the influences you allow into your life. Surround yourself with people who uplift and inspire you, people who share your values and encourage you to live your truest authenticity.

Distance yourself from those who seek to undermine your integrity or lead you astray from your true path. It does not matter the fact that you live in a world that is always on, you have the capacity to create your own world and that world will facilitate everything that happens to you or happens for you in this life.

When faced with moral dilemmas or ethical challenges, trust your inner compass - the voice of your conscience that whispers guidance in moments of uncertainty. Listen to that voice, honour its wisdom and let it be your guide as you navigate life's complexities.

Remember that living in integrity requires courage - the courage to speak your truth even when it is uncomfortable, the courage to stand up for what is right even in the face of opposition and the courage to be yourself unapologetically and authentically no matter the consequences.

Take note of the world around you; the cultural and traditional settings, the beliefs and paradigms of society, the injunctive norms placed on you that require you to live a certain way. That is a trap, it is the victim state where life only happens to you - it will look as if you have no control. I used to think that the people who are not privileged enough to be highly educated are the ones trapped in these injunctive norms, but no - there are people who are highly educated and still trapped in this conventional way of life.

There are many people who are financially solvent and still trapped in this conventional way of life – the injunctive norms placed on you by the society – living the beliefs, opinions and ideas of other people, trying to fit in to appease everyone. Please do not be trapped in this peer pressure called tradition. *"As for us, this is the way we do our things,"* so even if it is not within your capacity, even if you find no value in that you have to conform. You can never live your authentic self if you live in such a condition – peer pressure handed down to you by others. Avoid this pluralistic ignorance. This will force you to put up a public facade of a successful life while your soul bleeds.

Choose your own world, my dear. When you have the awakening to 'DO YOU', do not be afraid. That is the moment you realise you do not want to fit in anymore, you want to stand out - embrace this realisation. That is your moment to choose your world and live as you, no more existing but living. When the universe realises that you are willing, ready, and able to live authentically, then you will have the support you need to be you – you will suddenly become aware that you can shift your world. This is the point where purpose takes over pleasure, living intentionally and deliberately then become your focus.

Until the awakening, everything is normal to you. The moment you experience this awakening, you realise there is a world inside you that you want to experience and express. Many things that excited you in the past will not excite you anymore.

When you experience these moments, be careful of the people you share your experiences with. Many people go through life without experiencing this awakening and they will therefore see you as weird, backslidden, rebellious or overzealous. Gladly go through this experience, learning, relearning and unlearning and you will be amazed the transformation that will happen to your life. You will metamorphose.

Above all, know that you are not alone on this journey. Draw strength from the wisdom of those who have walked this path before you, people who have illuminated the way with their insights and inspiration. Seek out mentors, coaches and role models who embody the values you aspire to live by and let their examples guide and inspire you.

In the face of societal degradation and moral decay, it is easy to feel disheartened or disillusioned. Nonetheless, remember that you have the power to be a force for good in the world - to be a beacon of integrity, compassion and moral courage in a sea of darkness. Hold fast to your values, stay true to yourself and let your light shine brighter for all to see.

With Love and Solidarity.

Your Older Self,

Keziah

Dear Akosua Takyiwah, my Younger Self,

YOU CAN BE CLASSY AS A WOMAN ALTHOUGH IMPECUNIOUS

Being impecunious or having limited financial resources does not preclude one from embodying class and elegance. Classiness is not defined by material wealth but rather by one's demeanour, attitude and personal style. You are not a celebrity whose wardrobe is sponsored. Do not spend the money you will have to use to build a business or provide the needs of your children to dress to impress people. People do not care about you that much.

There are women who are wearing designer clothes, driving cars and living in houses they have no idea how much they cost. They come from families that are financially solvent. There are women who are very rich they can afford these things without robbing the bank. When your life is You, Yourself and Yours, you do not compete with others. Why on earth will you compete with such women? This competition is unhealthy.

Life is not about 'who' (designer) you are wearing. It is all about who is wearing what. Yes, money and luxury go hand in hand but being presentable, appearing decent and classy as a woman has nothing to do with luxury. Even if you do not shop for a straight two years, you can still dress up and be elegant from your old wardrobe. People wear expensive things and yet no one notices them because they lack confidence and character.

You can build your self-esteem so much that whatever you wear; you will stand out regardless of its price. Take note of the following on your quest to be classy without wasting money.

1. **Cultivate Confidence**: Confidence is the cornerstone of classiness. Carry yourself with poise and grace and embrace your unique qualities with confidence. Remember that true elegance comes from within. Walk gracefully with your head upright and chin up, looking forward and take calculated strides.

2. **Prioritize Personal Hygiene and Grooming**: Take care of your appearance by practicing good hygiene and grooming habits. Keep your hair clean and well styled. Maintain well-groomed nails – that is not long artificial nails; you can keep your natural short nails properly manicured. Ensure your clothing is neat and well fitted even if it is not expensive. Take good care of your skin, there are places and products that are bespoke for you at your level and budget. Do not follow your friends to their places. You do not have to use the products they use when you cannot afford them. There are many cost-effective ways to care for your body yourself. There are means by which you can learn about self-care and how to pamper yourself even at home.

Focus on Timeless Fashion: Invest in a few key pieces of clothing that are versatile and timeless. Choose classic styles and neutral colours that can be mixed and matched to create various outfits. Look for quality items within your budget.

3. **Accessorize Thoughtfully**: Accessories can elevate even the most basic outfit. Invest in a few high-quality accessories, such as a classic watch, a statement necklace or a stylish handbag to add flair to your look. Choose accessories that complement your personal style and can be worn with multiple outfits. Change your necklace and shoes and you will still look good in the same clothing or dress. Learn how to keep your clothing properly and to store your necklaces, shoes and bags appropriately. Sometimes, all you are paying for is the brand's name, nothing elegant about their products.

4. **Embrace Minimalism**: Adopt a minimalist approach to fashion and beauty. Focus on quality over quantity and prioritize simplicity and sophistication in your wardrobe and makeup routine. A few well-chosen pieces can make a stronger statement than an abundance of clutter.

5. **Practice Good Manners and Etiquette**: Classiness extends beyond outward appearance to how you conduct yourself in social settings. Practice good manners, be courteous and respectful towards others and demonstrate kindness and empathy in your interactions. It does not matter what you wear, if your mannerisms are poor you cannot appear deft. Be mindful of the people you mingle with especially those that come asking you about your personal issues. Just because they share theirs with you - without you asking them does not mean you should divulge yours.

Do not just regurgitate everything on your mind and do not be bothered when such people get under your skin. Be thrifty with your words. Some people are not worth your time and energy. Whether they do that deliberately or mistakenly be mindful of how you react and respond to such situations. Self-control is another aspect of courtesy that makes you appear refined and chic. Self-control in the midst of provocation is the litmus test for refinement. Handle difficult situations with tact and finesse. Ignore what needs to be ignored and address assertively what needs to be addressed. Cultivate the strength to control your emotions - that makes you powerful.

6. **Cultivate Intellectual Curiosity**: Classiness is not just about appearance - it is also about cultivating a well-rounded intellect and engaging in meaningful conversations. Read widely, stay informed about current events, cultural trends and develop your interests and passions. Feed your mind with glamour, whatever you feed your mind is what you reflect upon. Be mindful of what you listen to because with time that is what you will reverberate. Upgrade your mindset and network. Learn beyond your field of study.

7. **Focus on Inner Beauty**: Ultimately, true classiness radiates from within. Cultivate inner beauty by nurturing your mind, body and spirit.

Practice self-care, pursue personal growth and development and cultivate qualities such as kindness, compassion and authenticity. Improve on your character, character is like a perfume, the fragrance follows you wherever you go.

You can be assertive and still respectful. Treat people honourably not because they are honourable but because you are as a woman. Be a healthier and happier you. Live clean, eat healthy, exercise regularly and maintain a healthy lifestyle. There are many free fitness plans you can subscribe to and get the body shape that you can admire and enjoy when you are naked and in front of a mirror. It is not about being thin; it is about being healthy at your size.

By embodying these qualities and adopting a mindset of elegance and sophistication as a woman, you can exude classiness regardless of your financial circumstances. Remember that true classiness is not about flaunting wealth but about embracing grace, dignity and integrity in all aspects of life. Life is not that complicated. Do not complicate yours.

With much Love and Blessings.
From Your Older Self,
Keziah

Dear Younger Self,

REST FOR YOUR BODY, SOUL AND SPIRT – REST IS NOT A LUXURY BUT A NECESSITY

As I reflect on the journey that has led me to this moment, I am filled with a deep sense of gratitude for the lessons learned and the wisdom gained along the way. In the hustle and bustle of life, amidst the demands of being a woman, mother, and wife, I want to share with you the importance of finding the right kind of rest - rest that nourishes your body, mind and spirit, allowing you to flourish and thrive in every aspect of your life.

First of all, I want you to know that rest is not a luxury but a necessity - a vital component of self-care and well-being. In a world that often glorifies busyness over productivity, it is easy to overlook the importance of restorative rest. Nonetheless, I urge you to prioritize rest as an essential part of your daily routine, recognizing its power to rejuvenate, replenish and restore your energy and vitality. Rest is a state of physical, emotional and mental relaxation that allows our bodies and minds to recover from the stress of daily life. It is essential for our overall health and well-being - it is just as important as diet and exercise. Rest is an act of faith - it allows us to quiet ourselves before God and revive our minds, bodies and spirits.

Rest is vital for mental health, it increases concentration and memory, a healthier immune system and reduce stress, improve mood and even a better metabolism. Finding the right kind of rest begins with honouring your body's natural rhythms and needs. Listen to your body's signals and cues and give yourself permission to rest when you feel tired or depleted. Whether it is a short nap, a leisurely walk in nature or simply sitting quietly with a cup of tea, find moments throughout your day to pause, recharge and replenish your energy reserves.

Rest is not just about physical relaxation - it is also about nurturing your mind and spirit. Take time to engage in activities that bring you joy, inspiration and a sense of fulfilment. Whether it is reading a good book, meditating or pursuing a creative hobby, find ways to nourish your soul and cultivate inner peace and tranquillity.

In the midst of life's demands and responsibilities, remember to savour the simple pleasures and moments of beauty that surround you. Whether it is watching the sunset with your family, sharing a meal together or laughing with friends, cherish these moments and let them nourish your soul.

Above all, trust in the wisdom of your own intuition and inner guidance. You are the only one who knows what kind of rest your body, mind and spirit truly need. Listen to that inner voice, honour your needs and make self-care a priority in your life.

By finding the right kind of rest, you will nourish yourself from the inside out, enabling you to flourish and thrive as a woman, mother and wife. Allow me to explain to you details about rest and its kinds.

There are seven types of rest, namely; physical, mental, emotional, sensory, creative, social and spiritual. Each type focuses on a different aspect of our lives. By understanding the different types, you can identify areas of your life where you need to focus on rest and prioritize your self-care accordingly.

1. **Physical Rest**

Physical rest means taking a break from the physical activities that we partake in all day. We often think of rest as just lying down or sitting but physical rest includes both active and passive components. The passive component includes high quality sleep. While the active component involves activities such as:

- stretching
- taking a nap
- getting a massage
- taking short breaks
- going for a walk, and
- having great and satisfying sex

When we rest physically, we give our muscles time to repair and recover which helps us avoid injuries and reduces fatigue.

2. Mental Rest

Mental rest means taking a break from the constant mental stimulation that we face daily. We live in a world that is always on the move and it can be challenging to unplug and give our brains a break. Ways to incorporate mental rest into your routine include:

- turning off your phone
- staying off social media for a while
- scheduling breaks through out your day that reminds you to pause or slow down.
- meditating few minutes of peace away from the hustle and bustle of the day.
- setting aside few minutes of quiet time each day to give your brain some form of rest.
- practicing mindfulness, and
- simply taking a few deep breaths – breath works.

When you are suffering from a mental rest deficit, you might have trouble recalling why you entered a room or may lay down at night and find you are unable to quiet your racing mind as you lay down at night to sleep. When you rest mentally, you give your brain time to recharge, process information and store the valuable things that help you to stay focused, productive and alert.

3. Spiritual Rest

Spiritual rest relates to the fundamental need for belonging. Do not forget we are spirits with souls living in bodies. An individual experiencing a spiritual rest deficit may feel like he or she is just busy but not productive or purposeful. They work only for wages and salaries, feeling that their lives lack meaning. In these moments, you must find ways to become involved in a community or find a greater purpose via prayer and connecting with God and doing something worthwhile with your life. Any time you feel an unusual restlessness, know that your soul needs answers that only your maker can provide, connect with him through:

- meditating
- praying
- engaging in a spiritual practice that you enjoy
- spending time in nature
- spending alone time in worship, and
- volunteering for a cause that you care about

When you rest spiritually, you give yourself time to connect with your inner self and find meaning in your life, which helps you to stay grounded and fulfilled.

4. **Emotional Rest**

Emotional rest is a type of calm you feel when you are able to be real and authentic, sharing your inner experiences openly and genuinely. People suffering from emotional rest deficit may feel the weight of an emotional burden to suppress their feelings or please people. Take the mask off. Emotional rest can also mean taking a break from the emotional demands that you face every day. It can include activities like:

- spending time alone and appreciating the gift of life
- avoiding stressful situations
- talking to a trusted friend, counsellor or a professional therapist
- practicing self-care
- journaling, and
- spending time in nature

When you rest emotionally, you give yourself time to process your feelings. This helps you to maintain your emotional balance and avoid burnout. Emotional rest can be challenging because we often feel guilty for taking time for ourselves, we are good with taking care of everyone but ourselves. However, it is essential to remember that taking care of yourself is not selfish.

5. Sensory Rest

Sensory rest means taking a break from the constant sensory inputs that you face daily.

We are bombarded with noise, light and other stimuli all the time and it can be overwhelming. Sensory rest can include activities like:

- turning off the television
- closing your eyes for a while
- spending time in a quiet room
- taking a lukewarm bath
- listening to calming music, and
- practicing deep breathing

People experiencing a sensory rest deficit may feel energized and happy at the beginning of the day but become increasingly more agitated and irritable as the day progresses because of the constant hum of technology, an influx of sensory stimulation.

When you rest your senses, you give your body time to recover from the overstimulation that you experience, which helps you avoid sensory overload and reduce stress.

6. Social Rest

Social Rest means taking a break from the social interactions that you face daily. We are social creatures but socializing can be draining, especially for introverts. You do not have to be at every event or every meeting to prove your loyalty and commitment.

At a point in your life, you will have to find your "hood", if not you will be lost in the crowd. *"Lose as many people as you need to in order not to lose yourself, no one worth keeping in your life is worth you losing yourself,"* the words of Najwa Zebian. Social rest can include activities like:

- spending time alone
- avoiding some social situations/events
- spending time with close friends and family, those in your inner circle
- having a solo picnic, hike or lunch, or
- practicing self-care

Social rest does not necessarily mean cancelling all social interactions. It is the feelings you experience when surrounded by those who make you come alive – certainly not the whole crowd. To prevent a social rest deficit, you should cultivate more positive, supportive and meaningful relationships in your life.

When you rest socially, you give yourself time to recharge and maintain your emotional boundaries, which helps you avoid social burnout and stay connected with meaningful relationships.

7. **Creative Rest**

Creative Rest means taking a break from the constant creative demands that you face every day. We often feel like we need to be constantly producing and creating but this can be exhausting. Creative rest can include activities like:

- taking a break from work (utilise your vacation and annual leave periods)
- pursuing a hobby
- engaging in a creative activity that you enjoy (such as drawing, painting, knitting, cooking a special dish, etc.)

Creative rest is the rest an individual experiences when he or she is able to appreciate beauty in any form. It re-awakens a sense of awe and wonder. Going out in nature and creating inviting spaces with visually appealing and calming pieces of art in one's home and work spaces are some ways to enjoy creative rest. When we rest creatively, we give our minds time to explore new ideas, which helps us stay inspired and motivated.

You may be wondering how to inculcate all these into your busy schedule. It is ether we find a way or we create excuses. If we cannot take good care of ourselves, who else will do it right by us?

Incorporating all seven types of rest into your life may seem daunting but it is essential for your overall well-being. Consider the following:

1. **Schedule it:** make rest a priority in your life by scheduling time for each type of rest. Just like you schedule time for work or exercise, schedule time for rest.

2. **Be intentional:** be intentional about the type of rest you choose and make sure it aligns with what your body and mind need.

3. **Take breaks:** take short breaks throughout the day to rest your body and mind. Go for a short walk, meditate or just take a few deep breaths. Move from your office to another department just to say hello to the colleagues there. These you can do regardless of where you might be if only you are intentional about it.

4. **Set boundaries:** set boundaries around your time and energy. Learn to say no when you need to and do not be afraid to ask for help when you need it.

5. **Disconnect:** disconnect from technology and social media regularly to give your mind a break from constant stimulation.

6. **Experiment:** experiment with different types of rest to find out what works for you. Everyone's needs are different, so find what brings you peace and incorporate it into your routine.

7. **Make it a habit:** make rest a habit in your life. Incorporate it into your daily routine and make it a part of your self-care practice.

In conclusion, remember, rest is essential for your overall health and well-being. Incorporating all seven types of rest into your life may take time but it is worth it. By prioritizing rest, you will be able to live a more balanced and fulfilling life. Take a break, relax and give your body and mind the rest they deserve.

Embracing all seven types of rest is a lifelong practice that can help you live a healthier, happier and more fulfilling life. So take a break and rest up.

Above all my dear one, understand that you can work out, eat healthily, observe all these forms of rest, if you do not deal with the stuff that is going on in your head and heart, you will never be healthy. You are not lost; you are just going through a tough phase in life where your old self is gone and your new self is still in the making. You are in the middle of changing, be patient with yourself. Sometimes life becomes like a sitcom, full of difficulties, moments that make you scratch your head and wonder is this real? Sometimes life can be like a binge, you will have to watch series you never signed up for. All you can do in these situations is to keep on keeping on, taking one right decision one-step at a time.

With Much Love and Blessings.

Your Older Self,

Keziah

Dear Younger Self, Akosua,

TO LOVE AND BE LOVED

As I reflect on the journey that has brought me to this moment, there are truths I wish to impart to you—wisdom born of both joy and pain, lessons learned through the sometimes treacherous waters of love and relationships. In matters of the heart, I want to offer you guidance that I wish I had received when I stood in your shoes, torn between the conflicting advice of others and the yearnings of my own heart.

First and foremost, I want you to know that you deserve to be loved deeply and authentically - not just by anyone but by someone who sees you, cherishes you and celebrates you for who you are. Do not settle for a love that is one-sided, unfulfilling or based on compromise. You are worthy of a love that is reciprocal, mutual and unwavering - a love that uplifts and nourishes your spirit rather than depletes it.

It is easy to be swayed by the well-meaning advice of older people who may urge you to prioritize practicality and security over matters of the heart. They may tell you to choose a man who loves you even if you do not love him back in return - a man who offers stability, financial security or social status. I urge you to resist this advice for it denies you the opportunity to experience the depth and richness of true love.

Instead, follow the whispers of your own heart - the quiet voice that knows what it truly desires, even when it is difficult to admit. Choose a man who ignites a fire within your soul, whose presence fills you with joy, passion and a sense of belonging. Choose a man who respects and honours your autonomy, a man who encourages your growth and celebrates your dreams. A man who will create space for you in his vision for you to thrive and flourish as his woman.

In matters of love, trust your instincts and intuition - they are your most reliable guides in navigating the complexities of relationships. Listen to that inner voice even when it is drowned out by the opinions of others or clouded by doubt and uncertainty. Honour your own needs, desires and boundaries and do not be afraid to walk away from relationships that do not honour the essence of who you are.

Beware of the men who feel they can own you because of the material things they provide for you; men who think making a lot of money has transformed them into some ultra-masculine alpha males, that the number of zeros in their bank accounts have metaphorically spiked their testosterone count and just the idea of snuggling up their wallets is enough to make every woman fall at their feet.

It is when you cannot provide your financial needs as a woman that you see a rich man as a gift sent from heaven, the moment you are able to do these for yourself, you will find no value in that relationship. If all a man can offer you is money without character and leadership, girl run for your life.

Remember that love is not a transaction nor is it a matter of convenience or obligation. It is a sacred bond between two souls - a bond built on trust, respect and mutual admiration. Do not settle for anything less than a love that sets your soul on fire, that makes you feel seen, heard and cherished beyond measure. Many people will advise you to go for a man that can provide, protect and preserve you without them even understanding what goes into these. If you love yourself and take good care of yourself, your standards and requirements will signal to a man that you do not love him more than you love yourself, therefore he will know that in order to be with you, he must provide, protect and cherish you. To the typical primitive African if a man can financially take care of his woman, as they say, *"spoil her"* – that means he loves her. Well, inasmuch as there is no love without giving, if a person gives out of his abundance, it is normal to him, it might not mean love to him.

In addition, forget about a man's six-pack, six-feet height and his six-figure income. If he is not generous, compassionate, kind and thoughtful, you will struggle in your love life with him.

You must know who you are, what you want from a man, what you are prepared to do to make sure the relationship is successful and what you are willing to give of yourself in the relationship before you are ready to love and be loved in return. This will enable you to discern and distinguish between who is right for you and who is good enough.

Use your femininity to prove a man without him knowing. A woman cannot function at her highest level with a man who is not proven. Prove his self-control – if a man cannot discipline himself in singleness, he will struggle with staying disciplined in marriage. Prove his servant leadership heart by expressing your needs and watch his responses. Prove his energy with you by sharing your dreams with him. Watch his reactions if he is aligned with just whom you are or he has the capacity to embrace where you want to go – the process of your becoming. These will equally let you know whether you can please him or not.

As in the words of R. C. Blakes Jnr, the Senior Pastor of the New Home Family Worship Centre in New Orleans, Louisiana and Houston, Texas, *"The man will be the horse and the woman the cart. Why will a cart be connected to a horse going on a direction that is not her destination?"* Always remember that marriage is not the end of me and myself as majority are professing. Yes, marriage is the birth of *"we and us" – the sum total of both of you.*

You both bring your whole individual selves into this union and form a merger inclusive of all your dreams, aspirations, abilities and capabilities and this merger creates something that is bigger and better than the two of you would have accomplished individually.

Therefore, as a woman you matter, you have a role to play in this merger. Unfortunately, if the man cannot create a space for you in this union, you will lose your providential way despite your capacity.

In the end, the choice is yours to make - the choice to follow your heart, to honour your truth and to embrace the kind of love that sets you free. Trust in yourself, trust in the power of love and trust that the right man will come into your life at the perfect moment, ready to love you in ways you never thought possible. Do not forget every choice comes with its own ramifications.

With Love and Solidarity.

Your Older Self,

Keziah

Dear Younger Self, Akosua

DEVELOP AND DEPLOY THE WOMAN IN YOU WHETHER SINGLE OR MARRIED

As I reflect on the journey that has led me to where I am today, there are truths I wish I had understood earlier - wisdom born of both joy and struggle, lessons learned through the highs and lows of life. One of the most important truths I want to share with you is the importance of recognizing yourself as a woman before anything else; before becoming a wife, mother or anything else society may expect of you.

You are more than your roles and responsibilities. You are a woman with dreams, desires and aspirations that are uniquely yours. Your worth is not defined by your ability to fulfil societal expectations or meet the needs of others. Your worth is inherent, intrinsic and deserves celebration.

In the midst of life's demands and pressures, it is easy to lose sight of yourself - to prioritize the needs of others above yours, to sacrifice your own well-being for the sake of those around you. Nonetheless, I urge you to remember that you cannot pour from an empty cup. You cannot truly give of yourself if you neglect the woman within you. You are a woman before a wife and mother. If you refuse to nurture, develop and deploy the woman in you, if you refuse to make her happy, financially sound and connect her to God

- not just to attend religious meetings, if you refuse to make her healthy and strong and teach her how to de-stress, being a wife and mother will frustrate and depress you. Why? Happiness is internal to an individual. If you understand this concept, whether single or married, you will be a happy woman.

Take the time to nurture yourself and to honour your own needs, desires and passions. Invest in your personal growth and development, pursue your interests and hobbies and prioritize self-care and self-love. Cultivate a strong sense of self-worth and self-respect and do not be afraid to set boundaries around your time, energy and emotions.

Remember that your happiness and fulfilment are not dependent on your relationships or roles in life. They come from within; from embracing whom you are, embracing your womanhood and living authentically and unapologetically as yourself. You are worthy of love, respect and fulfilment simply by the virtue of being you.

As you navigate the complexities of life, do not lose sight of the woman within you. Embrace, celebrate and honour her in all that you do. Know that by nurturing the woman within you, you will find the strength, resilience and inner peace needed to navigate life's challenges and embrace its joys.

With Love and Solidarity.

Your Older Self,

Keziah

Dear Younger Self,

YOUR INSECURITIES DO NOT DEFINE YOU DO NOT ANSWER TO THEM

I hope this letter finds you well, perhaps at a time when you might be struggling with uncertainties and doubts about yourself. I know how overwhelming it can feel, grappling with insecurities especially when they start to affect your relationships. That is why I am writing to offer you some advice that I wish I had received when I was in your shoes.

First and foremost, know that you are worthy of love and belonging just as you are. Your insecurities do not define you and they certainly should not dictate how you interact with others. Understand that everyone has his or her own struggles and imperfections and it is okay to have insecurities. The important thing is how you choose to deal with them.

Instead of letting your insecurities consume you, try to confront them head-on. Take the time to reflect on where these feelings stem from and work towards addressing them. This might involve seeking support from trusted friends, family members or even a professional therapist - people you can trust. Remember, there is no shame in asking for help when you need it.

When it comes to your relationships, try not to let your insecurities sabotage them. Trust is the cornerstone of any healthy relationship.

Constantly doubting yourself or your partner can erode trust over time. Learn to communicate openly and honestly about your feelings and give your partner the chance to reassure you when needed. Remember that he chose to be with you because he see something special in you.

Above all, be kind to yourself. It is easy to be your own harshest critic but try to practice self-compassion instead. Treat yourself with the same love and understanding that you would offer to a dear friend facing similar struggles.

I know it is easier said than done, but trust me, taking steps to address your insecurities will not only benefit your relationships but also lead to a greater sense of self-confidence and fulfilment. You are stronger than you realize and you have the power to overcome any obstacle that comes your way.

Believe in yourself, dear younger self and never forget that you are worthy of love and happiness.

With Love and Encouragement.

Your Older Self,

Keziah

Dear Younger Self,

DEAL WITH YOUR TRUST ISSUES BEFORE THEY DEAL WITH YOU

I am writing to you from the future not to impart wisdom but to offer a piece of advice that I wish someone had shared with me when I was in your shoes. It is about trust or rather, the lack thereof, and how it can shape the course of your relationships.

You see, I understand why you are wary of trusting others. Perhaps you have been hurt before, maybe someone you once relied on betrayed you or perhaps you are just naturally cautious. Whatever the reason, I want you to know that it is okay to be guarded but it is also important to recognize when your trust issues start to overshadow everything else.

Trust issues can be like a shadow, always lingering in the background whispering doubts and insecurities into your ear. They can make you question the intentions of those closest to you, even when they have given you no reason to doubt them. While it is natural to want to protect yourself from getting hurt, constantly keeping your guard up can prevent you from experiencing the true intimacy and connection you crave.

You see, intimacy is built on trust. It is about being vulnerable with someone, knowing that they will honour and respect that vulnerability.

When you are constantly second-guessing their motives or waiting for the other shoe to drop, it becomes impossible to fully let down your guard and open up.

I know it is scary to let yourself be vulnerable, especially when you have been hurt umpteen times. Regardless, trust me when I say that the rewards far outweigh the risks. When you allow yourself to trust others, you will find that your relationships become deeper, more meaningful and more fulfilling.

That is not to say that you should trust blindly or ignore your instincts. It is important to be discerning and to listen to your gut. However, try not to let past hurts dictate your future relationships. Instead, approach each new connection with an open heart and a willingness to give others the benefit of the doubt.

I have seen a marriage that was the envy of everyone get destroyed because the husband could not accept and believe that his wife will not have an extra marital affair with her ex-lover should they meet even after marriage just because he was privy to the bond she had with her ex-lover. The sad aspect about this story was that the wife had not seen her ex-lover for all those ten years of her marriage, not even communicating on the telephone. To prove his suspicion, this husband went ahead to do a DNA and the results indicated that all the children he had with his wife over that ten-year period were his.

The insecurities and lack of trust were fed so much that even during sexual intercourse, when the wife enjoyed it; the husband questioned whether she assumed he was her ex-lover. The times she did not enjoy this beautiful communion [lovemaking] with her husband, he will question whether she had wanted it to be with her ex-lover - such torment and immaturity. Pathetically, this marriage could not evolve into the union they envisaged. Trust is knowing everything or something can go wrong, but you will work them out together as a team. The best thing in life is finding someone who knows all your flaws, mistakes and weaknesses and still thinks you are the right person to be with. The most dangerous person to be with is the one who will not love you right neither will he or she want to leave you too. Work on your insecurities, deal with your trust issues, they can destroy beautiful relationships - and it will have nothing to do with your partner.

Remember, trust is like a fragile flower, it requires care, nurturing and the occasional leap of faith. Do not let your trust issues prevent you from experiencing the beauty of true intimacy and connection. Your future self will thank you for it.

With Love and Understanding.

Your Older Self,

Keziah

Dear Younger Me,

FINANCIAL FREEDOM, FINANCIAL METANOIA IS GODLY. DON'T BUY INTO THE LIES AND MYTHS ABOUT MONEY

I hope this letter finds you well. I know you are full of dreams and aspirations, eager to carve out a life that is truly yours. I want to share some wisdom about financial solvency, which will empower you to live independently and confidently without depending and relying on others for your survival financially.

Financial solvency means having enough income to cover your expenses and having a safety net for emergencies. It is about making your money work for you, so you are not constantly at the mercy of financial uncertainty. Somethings are prayed for - you have been taught, right? Many other things are paid for. When your financial status changes, many of your prayers will be answered, you will be able to own your life and command respect. If you are "*broke*" as a woman, understand that marriage is not an *economic empowerment*; get your finances in check so you do not become a liability to your man. Just in the same spirit, you should *NOT* be with any "*BROKE*" man. In this era, even if you are a full-time homemaker, you can still make money. Being poor is; **P**assing **O**ver **O**pportunities **R**epeatedly. There are many opportunities all over. Consider these steps, adopt and adapt.

Steps to Achieve Financial Solvency

1. **Educate Yourself About Money**

- **Read Books and Articles:** Start with personal finance classics like Streamline, Financial Intelligence, and Self-Investment by Kwabena Obeng Darko. The School of Money, Hunger for Success by Dr. Olumide Emmanuel, Rich Dad Poor Dad by Robert Kiyosaki and The Total Money Makeover by Dave Ramsey. These will give you foundational knowledge. The person who buys books and does not read has no advantage over the one who does not have the books.

Do you know Mr. Obeng Darko? I call him Professor because of the mindset shift about entrepreneurship he is influencing in the African minds via social media, through his books and seminars.

- **Take Courses:** Online platforms like Coursera and Khan Academy offer free courses on personal finance, knowledge is power. Attend seminars and events by Mr. Obeng Darko. Do not just read; do not just acquire financial education, take action.

2. **Create and Stick to a Budget**

- Budgeting is not for the rich or poor. It is simply knowing what you are spending your money on instead of waking up to ask where your money went.

Many a time, it is not how much you earn that matters but how you spend your money. There are those that regardless of your budgeting, your expenses are more than your income so definitely you will struggle.

These expenses are not even the extras; they are the basic needs for your family and yourself. This simply means you need another source of income.

What service can you render? What needs can you meet? What questions can you answer? Out of these three scenarios, you can create an extra income.

- **Prioritize Needs Over Wants:** Ensure that your spending aligns with your priorities. Focus on necessities like housing, food, and savings before discretionary expenses. Use the following check list to guide you:

1. Do not spend more than you earn with the anticipation that you are going to get money soon. (Imaginary income)

2. Delay gratification instead of instant gratification. If it is not urgent and important, it can wait.

3. Understand that you are in charge of your financial status, until you do something about it, nothing about it changes.

4. When you are financially overwhelmed and seeking a way out of your situation, there is a gap between cynicism and hope. No one is coming to get you, arise and get to work.

3. **Build an Emergency Fund**

- **Save Regularly:** Aim to save at least three to six months' worth of living expenses. This fund will be your buffer in case of unexpected expenses or job loss. Savings is a culture not necessarily how much you save. What is important is to be consistent with it.

- **Automate Savings:** Set up automatic transfers to your savings account to make saving effortless. Many people will never save manually, therefore, let your bankers or your employers help you by automatically deducting or moving that money into savings or deducting from your salary directly by your employer into a different account. Whatever arrangements that can work for you.

4. Manage Debt Wisely

- **Avoid High-Interest Debt:** Stay clear of credit card debt. If you must use credit, pay off the balance in full each month.

- **Pay Off Existing Debt:** Use strategies like the debt snowball (paying off smallest debts first) or the debt avalanche (paying off high interest debts first) to eliminate debt systematically.

5. Invest for the Future

- **Start Early:** The power of compound interest means the sooner you start investing, the more your money will grow. You can as well find other means of saving not necessary a savings account. What side business can you do so you can invest a certain percentage of your salary into it monthly as you get paid.

- **Diversify Your Investments:** Do not risk everything on one endeavour – do not put all your eggs in one basket. Spread your investments across assets. Do not waste your money on liabilities.

Anything that does not bring you money is a liability no matter the prestige that comes with it. Focus on assets, what brings in money.

6. Increase Your Income

- **Develop Marketable Skills:** Invest in money mindset education and skill development. This could mean pursuing higher education, certifications or learning new technologies.

- **Side Hustles:** Explore side gigs or freelance work that align with your skills and interests. If you could be an intermediary to connect your friend with a lover, you can start a business regardless of your financial status. Your character, personality and honesty are all forms of capital you can rely on. Whenever you hear capacity do not just think money. Salary will only pay your bills; it is your hustles that build your legacy.

7. Live Below Your Means

- **Avoid Lifestyle Inflation:** As your income increases, do not fall into the trap of increasing your spending proportionally – *keeping up with the Joneses*. Save or invest the extra income instead. When you are on a quest for financial freedom, your life is not supposed to make sense to anyone.

- **Minimalism:** Embrace a minimalist lifestyle by focusing on experiences and relationships over material possessions. I hope you are aware as I said in one of my earlier letters to you. Many a time, we are only paying for the brand's name, nothing elegant about their products.

8. Plan for the Long Term

- **Set Financial Goals:** Have clear, achievable financial goals for the short, medium and long term.

  Have a well-defined financial goals - in the next five, ten and twenty years, where do you want your financial status to be? Do you have family financial goals? What financial plan have you put in place for your children's education?

- **Regularly Review Your Finances:** Periodically review your financial situation and adjust your plan as necessary. Be in control of your financial future; do not buy into the *"whatever will be will be"* attitude. You are the architect of your fate. Nothing changes until you change something. You cannot live without a financial plan and expect to be financially free someday. An object will remain stagnant until force is applied.

Building the Right Mindset

Patience and Discipline: Financial solvency does not happen overnight. Be patient and stay disciplined, determined and dedicated.

- **Self-Reliance:** Trust in your ability to manage your finances. The more you learn and practice, the more confident you will become. Have you wondered why you keep wasting money until you are *'broke'* to get ideas on how to invest? The money in your hands will always be parallel to your mindset. When your mindset is Ten

Thousand Ghana Cedis (GH¢10,000), you cannot manage and regulate a Hundred Thousand Ghana Cedis (GH¢100,000). If you think it is someone else's responsibility to solve your financial difficulties for you, your brain will never get to work on how to breakthrough your financial struggles.

- **Seek Advice:** Do not hesitate to consult with those who have used our local system and structures to break through financially when needed. They can provide valuable insights and guidance. I am not talking about those born into wealth but those who created it from ground zero, they have a lot to teach and share.

- Did you know that money has actually left the offices; it is in the gutters now? Apart from your regular job, what else can you do to earn extra? What questions can you answer? What needs can your meet? What services can you render? Will these be with products or a service?

- You have the power to shape your financial future. By taking control of your finances now, you can build a life where you are not dependent on anyone else for support. You will be free to pursue your passions and dreams without the constant worry of financial instability.

Believe in yourself and your ability to achieve financial freedom. Your future self will thank you for the efforts you make today.

With Love and Blessings.

Your Older Self,

Keziah

LET RAISING WHOLESOME CHILDREN BE YOUR DESIRE

As you embark on the incredible journey of motherhood, I want to share some advice to help you raise wholesome, kind and resilient children. The path will not always be easy but it will be filled with joy, love and unforgettable moments. Here are some key principles to keep in mind. Raising wholesome children goes beyond financially providing for them, you will need to be present in their lives. If children go through attachment disorder in early years, all they aspire is to find love in wrong places and with wrong people. Many people are just trapped in toxic relationships today because they were encouraged to normalise dysfunctionality. These people have difficulty trusting others or feeling safe and secure in relationships, resulting in difficulty forming and maintaining friendships even romantic partnerships. They are hooked onto relationships that suck their lives away. Many others neglect every other thing and invest their time and efforts into building carriers, amassing wealth and acquiring many material things until they get to the top and yet they find no fulfilment. How children are raised affect their adult lives. Consider the following:

1. **Lead with Unconditional Love and Patience:** Every child is unique and will grow at his or her own pace. Shower them with unconditional love and be patient with their learning processes.

They will remember the warmth of your embrace and the kindness in your voice more than any specific lesson.

Make sure your children know they are loved unconditionally. This provides a strong foundation of security and self-esteem.

2. **Be a Positive Role Model:** Children learn more from what you do than what you say. Demonstrate the values you wish to instil in them—honesty, respect, kindness, empathy, etc. Let them see you practicing these values daily. Children learn by observing their parents. Therefore, demonstrate the behaviours you want to see in your children such as kindness, respect, honesty and patience and watch them exhibit them too.

3. **Foster Open Communication:** Create a home environment where your children feel safe to express their thoughts and emotions. Listen actively to their concerns and validate their feelings. This will help them develop confidence and emotional intelligence. Prioritize communication because open and honest communication is vital. Listen actively to your children's thoughts and feelings and encourage them to express themselves. This builds trust and ensures they feel heard and valued.

4. **Encourage Curiosity and Learning:** Nurture their natural curiosity by providing a stimulating environment. Encourage them to ask questions, explore new interests and embrace learning as a lifelong journey. Celebrate their achievements and support them through their struggles.

5. **Set Clear Boundaries and Be Consistent:** Establish clear rules and expectations and be consistent in enforcing them. Children thrive with structure and knowing the boundaries within which they can safely operate. Be firm but fair and explain the reasons behind the rules. Children need structure to feel safe. Establish clear rules and consequences and be consistent in enforcing them. Consistency helps children understand expectations and develop self-discipline.

6. **Teach Resilience:** Life will present challenges; it is important for children to learn how to cope with setbacks. Encourage them to view failures as opportunities for growth and to develop problem-solving mindset. Be there to support them but also allow them to navigate difficulties independently.

7. **Promote Healthy Habits:** Instil the importance of physical health through nutritious eating, regular exercise and adequate sleep. Additionally, emphasize the importance of mental well-being by encouraging mindfulness, stress-relief activities and a balanced approach to life.

8. **Create Family Traditions:** Build strong family bonds through shared activities and traditions. Whether it is a monthly prayer time, holiday rituals or regular family meals, these moments will create lasting memories and a sense of belonging.

9. **Emphasize Gratitude and Giving:** Teach your children to appreciate what they have and to give back to others.

Encourage them to practice gratitude daily and to participate in acts of kindness. This will help them develop a generous spirit and a positive outlook on life.

10. **Be Gentle with Yourself:** Remember, you are learning and growing alongside your children. It is okay to make mistakes and to ask for help when needed. Take care of your own well-being, as a happy and healthy parent is the cornerstone of a happy and healthy family.

11. **Encourage Independence**: Allow your children to make choices and take on responsibilities appropriate for their age. This fosters independence and self-confidence. Support their efforts and provide guidance when needed.

12. **Spend Quality Time Together**: Dedicate regular, uninterrupted time to engage in activities your children enjoy. This strengthens your bond and creates lasting memories.

13. **Teach and Practice Empathy**: Encourage your children to understand and respect the feelings and perspectives of others. Model empathetic behaviour in your interactions with others.

14. **Promote a Growth Mindset**: Encourage your children to view challenges as opportunities for growth rather than obstacles. Praise their efforts and resilience not just their achievements.

The teenagers have their own challenges, they do not have the privileges of children nor the rewards of adults and it is confusing and frustrating for them, be patient with them.

15. **Support Emotional Development**: Help your children recognize and manage their emotions. Teach them healthy ways to cope with stress and express their feelings constructively.

16. **Take Care of Yourself**: Maintain your well-being by taking time for self-care. A healthy and balanced parent is better equipped to take good care and support their children - do not neglect yourself.

17. **Adapt Your Parenting Style**: Be flexible and adjust your parenting approach as your children grow and their needs change. What works for a toddler will definitely not be suitable for a teenager.

18. **Seek Support When Needed**: Do not hesitate to reach out for help or advice from friends, family or professionals. Parenting is challenging and seeking support is a sign of strength not weakness.

Building a healthy relationship with your children is a continuous process that involves patience, understanding and love.

By integrating these principles into your daily interactions, you create a nurturing environment that supports your children's development and strengthens your relationship.

Raising wholesome children is a beautiful and rewarding endeavour. Trust your instincts, cherish the moments and believe in the incredible potential within your children.

With Love and Encouragement.

Your Future Self,

Keziah

Dear Akosua, my Younger Self,

IF YOU WANT TO OWN YOUR LIFE, MOVE AWAY FROM THE SENSE OF ENTITLEMENT

I hope this letter finds you well. As I reflect on my journey and the lessons I have learned along the way, there is one important piece of advice I would like to share with you; beware of the entitlement mentality, you can never own your life and live on your own terms if you allow other people to drive your life. Be on the driver's seat and take charge.

Entitlement mentality is defined as a sense of deservingness of a favour when little or nothing has been done to deserve a special treatment. It is the *"you owe me"* attitude. Entitlement is a narcissistic personality trait. It is not known exactly how this mentality develops. It may be due to social factors like:

- The environment people grew up in
- The way parents treated their children - the spoilt child syndrome
- Whether adults solved all their children's problems, and
- How people are treated by authority figures and significant others in their lives.

The environment one is raised in can affect how they see the world and what they expect from other people. It can even affect personal and professional relationships.

A sense of entitlement can sometimes be a symptom of a personality disorder. These disorders affect how a person sees themselves as well as others. Narcissistic personality disorder (NPD), antisocial personality disorder (APD) and borderline personality disorder (BPD) are a few conditions that may contribute to a sense of entitlement.

How the Entitlement Mentality affects Relationships and Mental Health

People with an entitlement mentality often see themselves as superior to others. It is no surprise that this way of thinking affects interpersonal relationships.

Long-term damage. When you believe you are entitled to better treatment than others or the rules do not apply to you, you are more likely to suffer in the long term, given that you simply believe you are not getting what you are owed. An entitlement mentality can result in:

- Conflict in relationships
- Unhappiness
- Disappointment, and
- Depression

Your career may suffer too. Entitled people often interview well and can land leadership roles because of their confidence.

However, they often lack team spirit and avoid problem solving in the workplace. Most of the decisions an entitled person makes are self-serving. This can quickly become apparent to their co-workers.

The Cycle of Entitlement

Feeling entitled to something and the disappointment that follows when you do not get what you want can reinforce entitled behaviour. This typically follows a vicious three-step cycle:

- When you are entitled, you are always vulnerable to the threat of unmet expectations.
- When your expectations are not met, it can lead to dissatisfaction and other emotions like anger and a sense of being cheated.
- When you are distressed, you try to fix the situation and console yourself. This results in self-reassurance that you deserve everything you have ever wanted, which reinforces the same entitled behaviour.

What an entitled person is like

Demanding special treatment, expecting other people to do things for them without showing gratitude and the need for constant admiration are a few characteristics of people with a sense of entitlement. Such behaviour can stem from upbringing or personality disorders and can be devastating for relationships.

A sense of entitlement is a personality trait based on the belief that one deserves special treatment or recognition for something they did not earn. People with this mindset believe that the world owes them without giving anything in return.

People with a sense of entitlement think they deserve special treatment. Their view is *"the world owes me."* They expect to elevate their lifestyle above that of others without putting in the effort needed to do so.

Entitled people feel like others should do things for them because of their connection to them or how much money or power they have. If they have reached a certain level of success, they feel that everyone should bend over backward to help them. They believe that it is other people's job to ensure they have everything they need even if this means that these other people do not have time to take care of their own responsibilities. Entitled people often act like **victims** and blame other people or outside forces for their problems.

Some entitled people secretly struggle with insecurity. While the person with a sense of entitlement may come across as **arrogant** or confident, this can be a cover-up for underlying insecurity or fear of not having enough admiration, resources or support. This fear and insecurity can also appear alongside **depression** and self-isolation.

Tips for overcoming a Sense of Entitlement

It is not always easy but it is possible for people with a sense of entitlement to overcome this feeling and adopt new behaviours in order to achieve their goal of being more independent.

Here are a few suggestions to overcome a sense of entitlement.

1. Recognize the Feeling of Entitlement

Refuse to let the feeling of entitlement affect your life. If you have a hard time recognizing the feeling, think about other times when you felt entitled and then notice how much that feeling resembles what you feel at a given time.

2. Understand That You are Not Entitled to Anything

Unfortunately, the world does not owe anyone anything. Sometimes life seems unfair and it is our job to make the best of what we get in life. We should not complain about what we deserved and never got – what we never worked for but thought it should have come to us because we deserve it.

3. Give Without Expectations

Find ways to help others without expecting anything in return. How can you serve others without expecting anything in return? Simple: volunteer your time and efforts and see your giving as charitable.

If you want something in return for your services, have the needed conversation, do not assume anything. If you are not giving for the sake of charity then be careful because very soon you will bleed. You can consider your services as giving back to humanity and enjoy the *"happiness"* from knowing that you have helped those less fortunate than yourself.

4. Distinguish Between Needs and Wants

Learn the difference between needs and wants. People with a sense of entitlement have a problem distinguishing between needs and wants. This makes it very difficult to make healthy and sound decisions since they constantly want more than they need. Instead, focus on what you truly need in life and cut out what you simply want.

5. Focus on Things You Can Control

Focus on what is in your control rather than what is not. You can only control your own thoughts, feelings, actions and responses. Stop focusing on what other people are doing or how they are responding to situations. Instead, focus on changing the things in your life over which you have some influence.

6. Cultivate Gratitude

Practice gratitude for every good thing in your life, no matter how small or insignificant it may seem at the time. Consider everything you have in your life right now: a home, family or friends, good health, etc. Take a moment to be grateful for everything that you have and realize that there are many people out there who would love to trade places with you.

7. Think of Others

Think about how your sense of entitlement affects other people in your life. Have you unintentionally made them feel guilty or resentful because they did not live up to your expectations? If so, remember that other people have their own lives to live and their own emotions to grapple with.

8. Show Yourself Kindness

Take good care of yourself and be kind to yourself because nobody else will do it right by you. It might seem counterintuitive but one way out of self-entitlement is to be kinder to yourself. When you are feeling entitled, it can be difficult or impossible for you to take care of your own needs. Instead, you might fall into a place of self-neglect because you are expecting others to take care of you.

9. The golden rule

Practice the act of treating others the way you would like to be treated. Regardless of social status, we are all humans after all.

10. Recognize that not all situations are unfair

If you find yourself in a seemingly unfair situation, pause for a minute and think about the greater good. For example, will it be right to assume that you must get good grades because you pay for an expensive tuition despite the fact that you do not study well enough? Consider what the school setting would be like if a student does not need to work for good grades. Consider getting a promotion just because you have worked at a place long enough, regardless of your contribution to the organisation. If the organisation was yours, will that sit well with you?

11. Respect

Exhibit respect and kindness when interacting with others. Every person has emotions and struggles to deal with, go easy on others. Be sympathetic to the needs of others. Just because some people do not publicise or talk about their challenges does not mean all is rosy with them. Some of those you think and believe should attend to your needs need more support than you could ever imagine.

How to deal with entitled people

It can be challenging to deal with people who seem entitled and selfish. Such relationships can create stress and wear on your own sense of self-worth. Some steps you can take to protect yourself and deal with entitled people include:

Boundaries

Clearly explain your **boundaries** and then call people out if they violate them. Let them know that the behaviour is unacceptable and that you will not be able to engage until they adopt a less harmful attitude.

a) Practice saying "No"

If someone is making excessive, unrealistic demands, do not be afraid to say no. Set limits on what you are willing to accept and be willing to deny their requests if they are asking for too much.

b) Encourage them to problem-solve

If someone demands that you solve their problems, encourage them to seek solutions independently. You might do this by saying, *"I'm not able to do that, but let's think of what might help you do this."* Encouraging people to look for ways to help themselves can foster greater self-sufficiency.

Remember, making any sort of change is not always an easy journey. Nevertheless, it is one that will be worth it. If you have trouble navigating these changes on your own consider reaching out to a mental health professional for guidance, they can help you discover the root of issues that have led to a sense of entitlement or teach you how to deal with an entitled person who is sucking the blood out of you. It is essential to understand that seeking help from a therapist or a professional counsellor is not a sign of weakness.

Instead, it is a sign that you have identified a need to change and that you wish to improve your life and relationship with others for the better. Over time, you can learn ways to address issues of entitlement and how to live a healthy and balanced life.

Overcoming a Sense of Entitlement

Do not take it lightly when people disrespect you because they have to feed you, cloth you and pay your bills. Until you rise up and take hold of your life, you will think you cannot be an independent fellow. Reconnect with yourself, own your life and live on your terms.

Let me conclude with this story. In the early years of Napoleon Bonaparte, he said and I quote *"God is on the side of the biggest artillery."*

Years later, when he was exiled on an island, he reversed his opinion and conceded, *"Man proposes but God disposes."* Many a time, you put in so much hard work, pray so much well, do everything humanly possible yet your results do not reflect your efforts. Various people then come your way with all kinds of advice as if you have no brains. Yes, I do understand that scenario very well. All I am saying is; keep on keeping on, continue investing into your life for it is the end of a man that matters not when he is going through his process of life.

There are people you expect to help you in one way or the other and yet they are indifferent toward your situation; you cannot force anything out of anyone. Just let the universe acknowledge that you are ready and willing to own your life and watch the assistance that will come from strangers.

With Best Regards.

Your Older Self,

Keziah

Dear my Younger Self,

DO NOT EXPECT A MONOGAMOUS RELATIONSHIP FROM A MAN WHO IS POLYGYNOUS

I hope this letter finds you in good health and high spirits. As I sit down to write this, I think about the journey you are about to embark on and the lessons that await you. There is one important guide I want to share with you - something that will save you heartache and guide you towards healthier relationships.

You may soon find yourself captivated by a man who practices polygyny and while his charm and attention may be intoxicating, it is crucial to recognize and respect the reality of his lifestyle. You may be dating him right now and all your quarrels have to do with his multiple choice of women aside his relationship with you. You might have even ended the relationship several times with him because of this lifestyle. Do not think marriage will change him. Polygyny, where a man has multiple wives or partners is a commitment he has chosen and it comes with its own set of beliefs and expectations that differ significantly from those of a monogamous relationship. You have heard the saying every man cheats, right? Well, that is not entirely true. A man can love multiple women from his heart for various reasons but when a man loves you from his soul, you are enough for him. Monogamy used to be one person for life, but it seems it is now one person at a time.

When you say, *"I love you,"* and a man responds, *"I love you too,"* understand that you are talking about two different expressions of love. Love has many subtleties and it means different things to different people at different stages of their lives.

You may hope that your love and devotion will be enough to change a man's ways or that he might choose to be monogamous for you. However, this is a path fraught with disappointment. It is not about your worth or the strength of your love - it is about understanding and accepting the choices that others make for their lives and understanding vividly that you equally have the right to choose the life that you equally want too. Always remember that when someone decides to be audacious with their disrespect, you have the common sense to be courageous with your boundaries for your sanity and growth. You do not owe kindness to a person who treats you with contempt. You can mean nothing to someone that means the world to you.

Entering a relationship with someone who practices polygyny means accepting that you will not be his only partner. This can lead to feelings of jealousy, inadequacy and emotional strain if you do not have the capacity for such. This can be avoided by aligning yourself with someone whose values and relationship goals match yours.

Here are a few things to keep in mind:

1. **Know Your Worth**: You deserve to be in a relationship where your needs and boundaries are respected. Do not settle for less than you deserve.

2. **Communicate Openly**: If you ever find yourself in such a situation, communicate your feelings and expectations clearly. Understand his perspective and see if there is a common ground but do not compromise on what you truly want for your life.

3. **Seek Compatibility**: Focus on finding a partner whose vision of a relationship aligns with yours. Compatibility is the foundation of a strong and fulfilling partnership.

4. **Self-Respect**: Always prioritize your emotional well-being. A relationship should uplift you not cause you stress or make you question your self-worth.

5. **Move Forward with Confidence**: If you realize that a polygynous relationship is not for you, have the courage to walk away. There are many people out there who share your values and are looking for the same kind of commitment.

Remember, love should be a source of joy and strength not confusion and pain. Trust in yourself and your instincts and have faith that the right person will come along, the one who will cherish you, as you deserve to be cherished.

With all my Love and Wisdom from the Future.

Your Older Self,

Keziah

Dear my Younger Self,

A PERSON'S BELIEFS, PARADIGMS AND PERSPECTIVES ARE OF GREAT IMMPORTANCE

I hope this letter finds you well at a place where you are open to new perspectives. As you navigate the complexities of relationships and consider the future you want for yourself and your children, I want to share some insights about hypergamy and hypogamy - concepts that can significantly influence your choices and their outcomes. Which one of these will be news?

- A man marrying his house help or
- A woman marrying her gardener?

Regardless, it is the quality of the relationship you build that matters.

Hypergamy refers to marrying or forming a relationship with someone of higher social, economic or educational status. On the other hand, **hypogamy** involves partnering with someone of lower status in these areas. Both have their own sets of benefits and challenges and understanding them can help you make informed decisions that are best for you and your children.

Hypergamy

1. Stability and Security:

- Marrying someone of higher status can provide greater financial stability and security that is beneficial for you and your children. You can leverage his social networks and his social capital. This can lead to better living conditions, education and opportunities. Somethings are prayed for; many other things are paid for or acquired through one's network. Many a time it is not about money, a person's network and capacity go beyond his or her financial statutes.

2. Social Mobility:

- Hypergamy can offer you and your children access to broader social networks and opportunities for advancement. This can pave the way for a better quality of life and more opportunities for growth and success.

3. Learning and Growth:

- Being with a partner who has achieved a higher status can expose you to new experiences, knowledge and perspectives. This can be enriching for you personally and intellectually and it can set a positive example for your children.

Hypogamy

1. **Strength of Character**:

- Choosing a partner of lower status can highlight qualities like resilience, ambition and the ability to overcome challenges. These are valuable traits that can contribute to a strong and supportive partnership.

2. **Empathy and Understanding**:

- A hypergamous relationship often involves greater empathy and understanding, as both partners navigate different backgrounds and experiences. This can foster deep emotional connections and a supportive family environment.

3. **Shared Goals and Growth**:

- Collaborating with someone of lower status can create a dynamic of shared goals and mutual growth. Working together to improve your circumstances can strengthen your bond and provide a powerful example of perseverance for your children.

Considerations for Your Children

- **Role Models**:

- Whether you choose hypergamy or hypogamy, the key is the quality of the relationship. Your children will learn from the way you and your partner treat each other, handle challenges and support each another. A person's beliefs, paradigms and perspectives are of great importance.

- **Opportunities**:

- Hypergamy can offer more immediate access to resources and opportunities, while hypogamy can teach valuable lessons about hard work, resilience and the importance of character over status.

- **Emotional Environment**:

- The emotional health of your relationship is paramount. A loving, supportive and respectful partnership will benefit your children the most, regardless of social or economic status differences.

In making your decision, prioritize the qualities that matter most to you in a partner and the kind of life you want for your children. Reflect on what will bring you happiness, fulfilment and stability. Remember that a successful relationship is built on mutual respect, shared values and a commitment to each other's well-being.

Trust yourself and know that you have the wisdom and strength to make the best choices for your future. Embrace the journey with confidence and an open heart.

With All My Love and Best Wishes.

Your Older Self,

Keziah

CHAPTER TWO

LETTERS TO MY BROTHERS

Dear Mr. Man,

LET YOUR DESIRE BE TO LIVE INTENTIONALLY AND PURPOSEFULLY

I hope this letter finds you well and full of energy as you embark on your journey through life. I know you are wondering whether I have nothing for you at all. Actually, everything I have written to the woman is equally applicable to you; you know the opposite is equally true, right? As you stand on the brink of adulthood, ready to live your full life there are many choices and paths ahead of you. I want to offer some advice to help you navigate these choices, become a man of integrity and plan a future that aligns with your deepest desires and aspirations.

Be True to Yourself

First and foremost, always be true to yourself. Understand who you are, what your values are and what makes you happy. Your authenticity is your greatest asset. Never compromise your core values or principles for the sake of fitting in or pleasing others. True fulfilment comes from living a life that is aligned with your own beliefs and goals. Do not buy into the typical primitive African parlance *"Be a man"* in situations you know deep down, you do not have to confront and situations you do not have to bottle up. Certain situations will never go away until they are confronted though.

Embrace Responsibility

Taking responsibility is a key part of becoming a man. Own your actions, decisions and their consequences. This means being accountable not only to yourself but also to others. You are not grown up until you know how to communicate, apologise, be truthful and accept accountability without blaming someone else. Whether it is in your personal relationships, career or other endeavours, responsible behaviour will earn you respect and trust. Do not ever forget that men are not put on this planet to simply pay bills, stress and die. Men are to be loved and respected too. Men need to be cared for too and that can happen when you live with integrity.

Set Clear Goals

Having a clear vision for your future is crucial. Set both short-term and long-term goals that are specific, measurable, achievable, relevant and time-bound (SMART). These goals will serve as a roadmap, guiding your decisions and actions. Regularly review and adjust them as needed to stay on track.

Invest in Yourself

Investing in yourself is one of the best decisions you can make. This includes education, skills development and personal growth. Read widely, seek out new experiences and continually challenge yourself. The more you learn and grow, the more opportunities you will create for yourself. The more knowledge you acquire, the more your old self give way to your new information and knowledge.

Build Strong Relationships

Surround yourself with positive and supportive people who inspire and uplift you. Strong relationships are built on trust, respect and mutual support. Be selective about who you let into your inner circle and nurture those relationships that are meaningful and enriching.

Practice Discipline and Hard Work

Success in any endeavour requires discipline and hard work. Develop good habits and a strong work ethic. Stay focused on your goals, even when the going gets tough. Remember that perseverance and persistency often distinguish those who succeed from those who do not.

Plan for the Future

While it is important to live in the moment, planning for the future is equally crucial. Think about where you want to be in five, ten or twenty years ahead. Consider the steps you need to take to get there. This might include financial planning, career development or personal milestones. Having a clear plan can help you make informed decisions that align with your desired future.

Maintain Balance

A fulfilling life is one of balance. While pursuing your goals, do not neglect other important aspects of your life, such as health, relationships and personal well-being. Make time for hobbies, relaxation and the people you care about. A well-rounded life is a happy and sustainable one.

Be Open to Change

Life is unpredictable and plans can change. Be open to new opportunities and adaptable in the face of challenges. Flexibility and resilience are key traits that will help you navigate the vicissitudes of life.

Becoming the man you aspire to be is a journey that requires intentionality, effort and reflection. Trust in yourself and your abilities. With a clear vision and a commitment to your values, you will create a future that is both fulfilling and meaningful.

With all my Best Wishes,

Keziah

Dear Mr. Man,

FIND A WOMAN YOU LOVE WHO EQUALLY LOVES YOU AND IS WILLING, READY AND ABLE TO DO LIFE WITH YOU

I hope this letter finds you well and full of hope for the future. As you navigate the path of life, one of the most significant choices you will make is choosing a life partner. This decision will profoundly influence your happiness, well-being and success. I want to share some advice on choosing a woman who will love and respect you and with whom you can build a fulfilling life.

Understand the Importance of Mutual Respect

A strong and lasting relationship is built on mutual respect. Choose a woman who respects you for who you are - your values, dreams and individuality. Respect her in the same way. This mutual respect will create a foundation of trust and understanding that is essential for a healthy relationship.

Look for Genuine Love

You have been socialised to believe that it is a man that has to love. A woman is only to submit to her man's love, right. Genuine love is more than just a fleeting emotion; it is a deep, abiding connection that grows stronger over time. Find a woman who loves you for who you are not for what you can provide or achieve. True love is accepting each other's flaws and imperfections and supporting each other through life's ups and downs.

Shared Values and Goals

Having shared values and goals is crucial for a harmonious relationship. Discuss your beliefs, aspirations and visions for the future early on. Whether it is your views on family, career, lifestyle or personal growth, aligning on these aspects will help you build a unified life together.

Communication and Understanding

Effective communication is key to any successful relationship. Choose a woman who is open, honest and willing to communicate her thoughts and feelings. Be the same with her. Understanding each other's perspectives and resolving conflicts through respectful dialogue will strengthen your bond.

Support and Encouragement

Your partner should be your biggest supporter and cheerleader. Choose a woman who encourages you to pursue your dreams and stands by you during challenging times. Likewise, be her source of support and encouragement. Together you can achieve great things.

Emotional and Physical Compatibility

Emotional compatibility is essential for a deep and fulfilling relationship. Look for someone with whom you can share your innermost thoughts and feelings. Physical compatibility is also important as it fosters intimacy and closeness. Both aspects contribute to a strong and satisfying partnership.

Kindness and Compassion

A woman who is kind and compassionate will bring warmth and positivity into your life. Her empathy and understanding will create a nurturing environment where both of you can thrive. Choose someone who treats you and others with kindness and compassion.

Independence and Partnership

It is important to find a balance between independence and partnership. Choose a woman who is self-sufficient and has her own interests and goals but who also values and invests in your shared life together. This balance will allow both of you to grow individually and as a couple.

Family and Social Relationships

Pay attention to how she interacts with her family and friends as this often reflects how she will treat you. A woman who values her relationships and treats others with respect and love is likely to bring those qualities into your relationship.

Trust Your Instincts

Finally, trust your instincts; your intuition can often guide you in the right direction. If something feels off, pay attention to that feeling. Conversely, if being with her feels right and brings you peace and joy, you are likely to be on the right path.

Choosing the right partner is one of the most important decisions you will make in your life. It is a choice that will shape your future in profound ways.

Be patient, take your time and make this decision with care and thoughtfulness. The right woman will love and respect you and be a true partner in every sense of the word.

With All My Best Wishes,

Keziah

Dear Mr. Man,

YOU CAN BE BROKE AS A SINGLE MAN, PLEASE DO NOT TRY THAT AS A MARRIED MAN

I hope this letter finds you well and in good spirits. As you contemplate the future and the kind of life you want to build, I want to share some advice about financial stability, especially as it pertains to marriage. Being financially prepared before entering into marriage can spare you and your future family unnecessary struggles and stress. It is not about being rich but having a financial goal that can cater for your lifestyle and that of the family you will build. Here are some thoughts on why it is crucial to ensure you are not '*broke*' as a married man and how to achieve financial stability. There are voluminous research out there indicating that millennials are choosing financial stability over romance.

The Importance of Financial Stability

Financial stability is a cornerstone of a happy and healthy marriage. Money problems are one of the leading causes of stress in relationships and they can lead to conflicts and strains that might otherwise be avoided. By taking steps to secure your financial future, you can create a more stable and peaceful home environment. Just as I wrote to my younger self in the woman's letters about finances, I am repeating for emphasis. Somethings are prayed for; many others are paid for.

Planning and Preparation

1. Set Financial Goals:

- Establish clear and realistic financial goals for both the short term and the long term. These goals might include paying off debt, saving for a home or investing for children's education. Having specific targets help you stay focused and motivated. No one can attain financial stability with his salary; have a plan to create wealth outside your regular job. It is true that some people have high paying jobs but what that means is without any other investment, they cannot sustain their lifestyle should they lose their jobs. Harness your skill set, gifts and talents and monetise them. Financial freedom is not a wishful thinking, there must be a plan that defines your financial goals and how to achieve them.

2. Create a Budget:

- Develop a budget that tracks your income and expenses. This will help you live within your means and ensure you are saving for the future. A well-planned budget is a powerful tool for managing your finances effectively.

3. Save and Invest:

Make saving a priority. Aim to save a portion of your income each month and consider investing it to grow your wealth over time.

Having a financial cushion can protect you against unexpected expenses and provide a sense of security.

Building Financial Literacy

Understanding how money works is essential. Take the time to educate yourself about personal finance, including topics like budgeting, savings, investing and managing debt. There are many resources available from books and online courses to financial advisors who can offer guidance tailored to your situation.

Avoiding Debt

While some debts like a mortgage can be part of a healthy financial strategy, excessive debt can be crippling. Be cautious about taking on debt, especially high-interest debt from credit cards or loans. Focus on paying off any existing debt as quickly as possible.

Communication with Your Partner

Financial transparency and communication with your partner are crucial. Discuss your financial goals, habits and concerns openly. Working together as a team to manage your finances can strengthen your relationship and ensure you are both on the same page.

Earning Potential

Consider your earning potential and career prospects. Invest in your education and skills to enhance your employability and increase your income over time.

A stable and growing income is vital for achieving financial security. Having a job as a young man might be ok but let your focus be to establish your own business, a legacy for your children.

Emergency Fund

Build an emergency fund that can cover at least three to six months' worth of living expenses. This fund will provide a safety net in case of unexpected events like job loss or medical emergencies.

Living Within Your Means

Live within your means, regardless of your income level. Avoid the temptation to overspend or keep up with others. Financial discipline and frugality are keys to maintaining long-term financial health. Your life is not to make financial sense to anyone. Work through your plans.

Planning for the Future

Think about the future and plan for major life events, such as having children, buying a home or building a house and retirement. Each of these milestones requires careful financial planning and preparation.

Seeking Professional Advice

Do not hesitate to seek professional financial advice if needed. Financial advisors who have lived their advice are better. A person teaching business strategy who has not built even one business from scratch to thriving using our system and structures cannot understand your situation. You do not need theories; you need a person that has walked through his or her teachings to provide valuable insights and help you create a plan tailored to your circumstances and goals.

By taking these steps, you can avoid the unnecessary struggles that come with financial instability. Ensuring that you are financially prepared before getting married will not only benefit you but also create a more secure and harmonious life for you and your future family.

Remember, being financially stable is not just about avoiding struggles; it is about creating opportunities and a better quality of life for yourself and those you love. Take control of your financial future and you will be better equipped to handle whatever challenges come your way.

With All My Best wishes,

Keziah

Dear Mr. Man,

GREAT SEX IS A BY PRODUCT OF A HEALTHY RELATIONSHIP

I hope this letter finds you well and in good spirits. As you navigate the complexities of life and relationships, I want to share some thoughts on a topic that is both personal and significant: the importance of intimacy with a woman you truly love and the reasons why it is beneficial to avoid casual encounters that can waste your energy and emotional well-being.

Great sex does not just happen, you will have to create it and be intentional about it. When your woman continuously refuses you sex, that is not the problem that is a symptom that there are dysfunctionalities that must be addressed. Women like and enjoy sex too - sex is not a man's thing. That same woman you think does not like sex, does not enjoy sex can meet another man and her whole body will stand at ease with sexual arousal. Consider the following, sir.

The Value of Meaningful Intimacy

Sexual intimacy is a profound and intimate act that can deeply affect your emotions, self-esteem and overall well-being. When shared with a woman you love and respect, it can strengthen your bond and enrich your relationship. Here are some key benefits of saving this intimate part of yourself for someone special:

Emotional Connection

1. **Deeper Bond**:

- Making love with someone you genuinely care about creates a deeper emotional connection. This bond goes beyond physical pleasure, fostering a sense of closeness and trust that enhances your overall relationship.

2. **Emotional Fulfilment**:

Having sex with a person you love can be emotionally fulfilling and comforting. It is an expression of love and affection, reinforcing your commitment to each other and providing a sense of security and belonging.

Physical and Mental Well-Being

1. **Health Benefits**:

- A healthy sexual relationship can have various physical benefits, including reducing stress, improving sleep and boosting your immune system. When this intimacy is shared with a woman you love, these benefits are often amplified due to the emotional support and happiness that come with the relationship.

2. **Mental Health**:

- Engaging in intimate acts with someone you love can improve your mental health by reducing anxiety, increasing happiness and fostering a sense of contentment and satisfaction.

Ponder These Benefits of a Healthy Sex Life

- Better sleep.
- Regulated blood pressure.
- Immediate natural pain relief.
- Better immune system.
- Better heart health, possibly including lower risk for heart disease.
- Improved self-esteem.
- Increased libido.
- Overall stress reduction, both physiological and emotional.
- Increased intimacy and closeness to a sexual partner, and
- Decreased depression and anxiety.

Unfortunately, the average typical primitive African man thinks and believes that having sex with multiple women is a showmanship of masculinity and takes pride in the fact that he has *'slept'* with half of the ladies in his community. Sadly, all what he gets is a space to ease himself, nothing more. I do not dispute the fact that there are women in this generation who equally consider sex as a game, they equally do not get the benefits and satisfaction that being with a man they truly love brings.

Avoid These Negative Consequences

1. Emotional Turmoil:

- Casual sexual encounters can lead to emotional turmoil, feelings of emptiness and regret. Without the foundation of love and commitment, these experiences can leave you feeling unfulfilled and disconnected.

2. Disrespect And Undignified:

- Choosing to be intimate with someone you love reflects self-respect and dignity. It shows that you value yourself and your partner and that you view intimacy as something precious, not to be taken lightly. Do not disrespect your chosen partner and become undignified by getting involved in casual sexual escapades.

Building a Strong Relationship Not Just Having Sex

1. Trust and Loyalty:

- Being intimate with a woman you love fosters trust and loyalty in your relationship. It is a mutual exchange of vulnerability and affection that strengthens your partnership and builds a solid foundation for the future.

2. **Shared Experiences**:

- Sharing intimate moments with a loved one creates lasting memories and shared experiences that deepen your connection. These moments contribute to the unique story of your relationship and enhance your emotional bond.

Energy and Focus

1. **Preserving Your Energy**:

- Your energy is valuable. By choosing to share it with someone you love, you invest in a relationship that brings joy, fulfilment and growth. This focus can lead to a more balanced and satisfying life. In some few years to come, you will wish you never wasted your energy through sex with women who never mattered. Having sex and making love to the woman you love are two different things.

2. **Avoiding Distractions**:

- Casual encounters can be distracting and may lead you away from your goals and priorities. Maintaining a meaningful relationship helps you stay focused on what truly matters in your life.

Having sex by yourself through masturbation will not stimulate the release of as much oxytocin or other mood-boosting hormones as having quality sex with a partner in a loving relationship; this means a little less benefit when it comes to self-esteem and depression.

At most, you can enjoy physiological benefits like pain reduction, better sleep and regulated blood pressure.

When I watch women on social media equating having sex with men to that of using sex toys, I just feel sorry for them because they don't fully understand what they are talking about.

It is either they have not given in fully to loving and adoring a man that loves and adores them too or they have not dealt with their childhood traumas so the hatred they have for men has blinded their sense of judgement.

A man that loves a woman releases oxytocin not just testosterone during sexual intercourse with her. The woman equally releases oxytocin during sex. When this happens, they bond together. A man who does not love a woman but has sex with her only releases testosterone. A man that loves a woman will not just spread her legs and just thrust his penis into her until he releases. The way he looks into her eyes, the manner in which he holds her to himself and the things he tells her during sex cannot be matched by the use of the most sophisticated sex toy.

Emotional, physical and mental health issues can interrupt a woman's ability to enjoy a healthy sex life. Nonetheless, every woman should be able to enjoy sexual health if she so desires.

There are books on sex that purport that a woman's orgasm is her responsibility just like the man's is his responsibility.

This is not wholly true; the anatomy of a woman is completely different from a man's. A man can view sex as a different item on the agenda. To him, whatever problems the woman has or exists in the relationship can be worked out later, once he wants sex he must get his satisfaction. On the other hand, a woman will need to be connected emotionally with a free heart and relaxed mind to be able to have sex and enjoy it.

If you treat your woman right, you will enjoy good sex. Doing things, you know she enjoys spontaneously. You cannot be too frugal to find it a problem to spend money on your woman and expect good sex from her. It is not about how much, but the thoughtfulness. A woman's sexuality is wrapped up in two things.

- How she feels about herself
- How she feels about you

Making Thoughtful Choices

It is important to make thoughtful choices about your intimate relationships. Reflect on your values and what you truly want from a partner. Aim for relationships that uplift you, provide mutual support and enhance your overall well-being.

Intimacy is a powerful and beautiful aspect of human connection. When shared with a woman you love, it transcends physical pleasure and becomes a profound expression of your bond. It nurtures your emotional and physical health, strengthens your relationship and ensures that your energy is invested in something meaningful and enduring.

Choose to value yourself and your partner by reserving this special part of you for someone who truly matters. By doing so, you will experience the true depth and joy that meaningful intimacy can bring. You cannot abuse, ignore, demean, disrespect, violate or intentionally not value your woman and expect to have great sex with her.

With All My Best Wishes.

Yours Truly,

Keziah

CHAPTER THREE

LETTERS TO THE YOUNG MEN AND YOUNG WOMEN

THE YOUNG MAN

Dear Young Man,

EMBRACE A MEANINGFUL LIFE

Congratulations on reaching a significant milestone, a pivotal moment in your life where you are ready to take your life seriously and seek out a meaningful existence. This decision marks the beginning of a journey that while challenging, can be incredibly rewarding and fulfilling. Here are some pieces of advice to guide you as you embark on this transformative path. This decision is the foundation for a fulfilling and impactful life. These pieces of advice will help you navigate this journey and make the most of your potential.

Define Your Values and Goals

1. **Identify Core Values:** Reflect on what truly matters to you. Understanding your core values will guide your decisions and actions, helping you stay true to yourself.
2. **Set Clear Goals:** Establish short-term and long-term goals that align with your values. Clear goals provide direction and motivation and help you measure your progress. Where do you want your life to be in the next five, ten or twenty years?
3. **Write It Down:** Document your values and goals. This practice makes them tangible and serves as a constant reminder of what you are working towards.

Invest in Your Education and Skills

1. **Lifelong Learning:** Commit to continuous learning. Pursue formal education, attend workshops and seminars, read widely and stay curious. Knowledge and skills are powerful tools for personal and professional growth.

2. **Develop Marketable Skills:** Focus on acquiring skills that are in demand in your chosen field. This increases your employability and opens up opportunities for career advancement.

3. **Seek Mentorship:** Find mentors who can provide guidance, share their experiences and help you navigate challenges. Learning from others successes and mistakes can accelerate your growth.

Build Healthy Habits

1. **Physical Health:** Prioritize regular exercise, a balanced diet and adequate sleep. A healthy body supports a sharp mind and enhances your overall quality of life.

2. **Mental Health:** Practice mindfulness, meditation and stress management techniques. Do not buy into the idea that a man should and must be ok. It is okay to not be okay and admit it so you can work at it.

3. Do not hesitate to seek professional help if needed. Mental well-being is crucial for sustained success and happiness.

4. **Consistency:** Develop and stick to routines that promote productivity and well-being. Consistency is key to building and maintaining good habits.

Cultivate Strong Relationships

1. **Surround Yourself with Positivity:** Build relationships with people who inspire and support you. Positive influences encourage you to stay motivated and focused on your goals. Do away with brothers who have no idea what they are doing with their lives yet.

2. **Communicate Effectively:** Develop strong communication skills. Effective communication fosters understanding and cooperation essential for both personal and professional relationships.

3. **Give Back:** Engage in acts of kindness and support others on their journeys. Building a network based on mutual respect and assistance enriches your life and the lives of those around you.

Practice Financial Responsibility

1. **Budgeting:** Create and stick to a budget. Understanding where your money goes helps you make informed financial decisions and avoid unnecessary debt.

2. **Saving and Investing:** Save a portion of your income regularly. Consider investing to grow your wealth over time.

Financial stability provides the freedom to pursue your passions and goals.

3. **Live Within Your Means:** Avoid the temptation to live beyond your means. Financial discipline ensures long-term security and reduces stress. If the life you desire comes with more money, work for more money. You cannot be *'broke'*.

Pursue Purpose and Passion

1. **Find Your Passion:** Identify activities and causes that excite and makes you fulfilled. Pursuing your passions brings joy and a sense of purpose to your life.

2. **Make an Impact:** Seek ways to contribute to your community or make a difference in the world. A life dedicated to helping others is rich in meaning and satisfaction.

3. **Stay True to Yourself:** Follow your own path and make choices that resonate with your inner beliefs and desires rather than conforming to external expectations.

Embrace Challenges and Learn from Failures

1. **Resilience:** Cultivate resilience by embracing challenges and viewing failures as learning opportunities. Each setback is a chance to grow stronger and wiser.

2. **Adaptability:** Be flexible and open to change. The ability to adapt is crucial in navigating life's uncertainties and seizing new opportunities.

3. **Perseverance:** Stay committed to your goals, even when faced with obstacles. Perseverance is often the key differentiator between success and failure. With discipline and dedication, your dreams will come alive. Those who live a good life are not better than you are; they took better decisions and made better choices. Success lives clues, when you pay the price, the prize becomes automatic.

Taking your life seriously and striving for meaning is a noble pursuit that requires dedication, self-awareness and continuous effort. By defining your values, investing in your education, building healthy habits, cultivating strong relationships, practicing financial responsibility, pursuing your passions and embracing challenges, you can create a life that is fulfilling and impactful.

Remember, the journey is just as important as the destination. Enjoy the process, learn from every experience and stay true to yourself.

With Warm Regards And Best Wishes For Your Journey.

Best regards,

Keziah

Dear Young Man,

FEMINISM HAS NOT DONE ANYTHING TO THE AFRICAN WOMAN - SOCIETY HAS EVOLVED

I hope this letter finds you well. I wanted to take a moment to share some thoughts with you about a topic that often sparks a lot of debate and misunderstanding: feminism. I understand that you might have concerns about how feminism could affect relationships particularly the love and dynamics between a man and a woman. I want to assure you that feminism is not something to be feared or viewed negatively and it certainly will not diminish the love a woman has for you simply because she identifies as a feminist.

If I may ask, who is a feminist in the first place? The God who created the man equally made the woman and blessed them both. Should we confine women to the domestic sphere, while public life is reserved for only men even if some women equally qualify for such portfolios? Many of the women who advocated feminism and women's rights in the formative years were broken women who sent out wrong ideologies. Will you support and assist your sisters, nieces and aunties to rise to their full potential? Then you are a feminist too. Women who are disrespectful to men are not feminists they are rude people, just like men who are rude. If you find any woman who dislikes, despises or is strongly prejudiced against men, she is a misandrist not a feminist. It is just like a misogynistic person who hates or discriminates against women.

Feminism, at its core, is about equality and respect. It seeks to ensure that women have the same rights, opportunities and freedoms as humans. This movement is about creating a world where everyone, regardless of gender, can thrive and be treated with fairness and dignity. Feminism does not advocate the superiority of women over men nor does it seek to undermine the love and respect that are fundamental to any healthy relationship.

Here are a few reasons why feminism should not be seen as a threat but rather as a positive force that can enrich your relationship:

1. **Mutual Respect and Equality**: Equality is important but I find equity attractive though. We cannot give the same every time but we can give wholeheartedly depending on our capacity every time. A feminist relationship is built on mutual respect and equality. When both partners see each other as equals, they are more likely to communicate effectively, support each other's dreams and share responsibilities. This creates a strong foundation for a loving and lasting relationship.

2. **Empowerment and Independence**: Feminism empowers women to be independent and confident. An empowered woman who feels respected and valued is likely to bring those positive qualities into her relationship.

Her independence does not mean she loves you any less; rather, it means she brings her full self into the relationship, enriching it with her strength and confidence.

3. **Shared Responsibilities**: Feminism encourages the sharing of responsibilities, whether they are financial, domestic or emotional. This sharing fosters a sense of partnership and teamwork, making the relationship more balanced and harmonious. When both partners contribute equally, it alleviates stress and promotes a supportive environment.

4. **Healthy Communication**: Feminist principles emphasize the importance of open and honest communication. In a relationship, this means discussing feelings, needs and concerns without fear of judgment or dismissal. Good communication is key to resolving conflicts and understanding each other better, strengthening the bond you share.

5. **Personal Growth**: Being in a relationship with a feminist can inspire personal growth. You will learn to see the world from different perspectives, challenge traditional gender roles and develop a deeper understanding of what it means to be an ally. This growth can lead to a more fulfilling and enlightened relationship.

It is important to remember that love is about accepting and appreciating each other for who you are. A woman who is a feminist loves just as deeply and passionately as anyone else.

Her belief in gender equality is not a barrier to love but a pathway to a more just and harmonious relationship.

Embrace the principles of feminism with an open heart and mind. You may find out that not only does it strengthen your relationship but it also enriches your own understanding of what it means to be a supportive and loving partner. Do you know your children take after the intelligence of their mother? Science has traced the "intelligence genes" to that of the X chromosomes and that children are more likely to inherit intelligence from their mothers because intelligence genes are located on the X chromosomes and mothers have two. Choose an empowered woman. A truly empowered woman knows the difference between being a woman and being a wife.

Wishing You All The Best In Your Journey Together.

Warm Regards,

Keziah

Dear Young Man,

PREPARE MENTALY AND EMOTIONALLY FOR MARRIAGE

I hope this letter finds you well. As someone who cares about your well-being and future happiness, I wanted to share some thoughts on the mental fortitude and emotional intelligence that are essential to cultivate before embarking on the journey of marriage. Marriage is a beautiful and fulfilling union but it also comes with its own set of challenges and demands. Preparing yourself mentally and emotionally can make a significant difference in building a strong and enduring relationship.

Mental Fortitude

1. **Resilience**: Life is full of ups and downs, and marriage is no different. Developing resilience means learning to bounce back from setbacks and not letting difficulties erode your spirit or commitment. This involves a positive mindset; the ability to adapt to change and the determination to keep moving forward even in tough times.

2. **Patience**: Patience is crucial in marriage. There will be times when things do not go as planned, when misunderstandings occur or when your partner needs more time to process her thoughts and feelings; you will need patience.

Cultivating patience helps you to handle these moments with grace and prevents impulsive reactions that can cause unnecessary harm.

3. **Commitment**: Understanding that marriage is a long-term commitment is vital. It is about sticking together through thick and thin and working through problems rather than walking away from them. This requires a deep sense of responsibility and dedication to making the relationship work, even when it is challenging.

Emotional Intelligence

1. **Self-awareness**: Being in tune with your own emotions, strengths, weaknesses and triggers allow you to manage your reactions and behaviours more effectively. Self-awareness helps you understand how your actions influence your partner and enables you to take responsibility for your own emotions rather than projecting them onto others.

2. **Empathy**: Developing the ability to understand and share your partner's feelings is key to a healthy relationship. Empathy allows you to see things from their perspective, validating their experiences and emotions. This fosters deeper emotional connections and reduces conflicts.

3. **Communication**: Effective communication is the backbone of any successful marriage. This means not only expressing your own thoughts and feelings clearly and respectfully but also actively listening to your partner. Good communication involves being open, honest and willing to discuss both the good and the difficult topics without fear of judgment.

4. **Conflict Resolution**: Every relationship encounters conflict. The ability to resolve disagreements constructively and without hostility is essential. This involves staying calm, avoiding blame, finding common ground and seeking solutions that satisfy both parties. Learning to compromise and let go of the need to always be right can prevent many conflicts from escalating.

5. **Emotional Regulation**: Being able to manage and regulate your emotions, especially during stressful times, is critical. This includes recognizing when you are feeling overwhelmed, taking a step back if needed and finding healthy ways to cope with stress and anger. Emotional regulation helps maintain peace and stability within the relationship.

Marriage is a partnership that requires effort, understanding and growth from both individuals. By developing mental fortitude and emotional intelligence, you equip yourself with the tools needed to navigate the complexities of married life.

Remember that this is an ongoing process—no one is perfect and there is always room for improvement. As you prepare for this important chapter in your life, take the time to reflect on these areas and work on strengthening them. Doing so will not only benefit your future marriage but also enhance your overall well-being and personal development.

Wishing you all the best in your journey towards a fulfilling and harmonious marriage.

Warm Regards,

Keziah

Dear Young Man,

HOW WILL YOU CHOOSE A HELP MEET WITHOUT KNOWING YOUR PURSPOSE?

I hope this letter finds you in good health and high spirits. As you stand on the threshold of an exciting chapter in your life, I want to share some thoughts with you about the importance of finding and living your purpose before you consider marriage. Understanding and embracing your purpose is not only crucial for your personal fulfilment but also significantly affects the kind of partner who will complement and support you in your journey.

Discovering Your Purpose

1. **Self-Reflection**: Take the time to reflect on your passions, strengths and values. What activities make you feel most alive and fulfilled? What are your natural talents and how can you use them to contribute to something greater than what you do? Understanding what drives you is the first step toward discovering your purpose.

2. **Setting Goals**: Once you have a clearer sense of your passions and strengths, set specific and achievable goals that align with your purpose. These goals will serve as a roadmap, guiding your actions and decisions.

Remember, your purpose is not just about career aspirations but also about how you want to impact the world and the legacy you wish to leave.

3. **Pursuing Growth**: Embrace a mindset of continuous growth and learning. Seek out opportunities to develop your skills, expand your knowledge and challenge yourself. Surround yourself with mentors and like-minded individuals who inspire and motivate you. Be careful of mentors who become tormentors. Personal growth is a lifelong journey that enriches your purpose.

Living Your Purpose

1. **Authenticity**: Live authentically by aligning your daily actions and decisions with your purpose. This means staying true to your values and passions even when faced with challenges or societal pressures. Authenticity attracts the right people into your life, including a partner who respects and supports your true self.

2. **Balance**: Strive for a balance between pursuing your purpose and maintaining other aspects of your life such as relationships, health and leisure. A well-rounded life ensures that you remain grounded and fulfilled, preventing burnout and fostering overall well-being.

3. **Contribution**: Use your purpose to make a positive impact on others. Whether through your work, community involvement or personal interactions, strive to contribute meaningfully to the lives of those around you.

This sense of contribution not only enhances your purpose but also creates a supportive and loving environment for a future partner.

Finding the Right Partner

1. **Shared Values and Vision**: Your purpose will naturally guide you towards someone who shares similar values and life vision. When both partners have aligned values and goals, it creates a strong foundation for mutual understanding, support and growth.

2. **Support and Encouragement**: The right partner will support and encourage your purpose, rather than compete with or diminish it. She will appreciate your dedication and be willing to make sacrifices when necessary, knowing that your purpose contributes to your overall happiness and fulfilment.

3. **Complementary Qualities**: Your purpose will help you identify the qualities that are most important in a partner. Look for someone whose strengths and interests complement yours, creating a balanced and harmonious relationship where both individuals can thrive.

4. **Emotional and Intellectual Connection**: A deep emotional and intellectual connection is essential for a fulfilling marriage. When you are living your purpose, you are more likely to attract someone who resonates with your aspirations and engages with you on a meaningful level.

Before embarking on the journey of marriage, it is crucial to have a clear understanding of who you are and what you want out of life. Finding and living your purpose provides a strong sense of direction and fulfilment, which in turn helps you attract a partner who is aligned with your values and goals.

Take the time to explore your passions, set meaningful goals and live authentically. By doing so, you will not only enhance your own life but also create a solid foundation for a successful and fulfilling marriage. It does not matter the capacity of the woman you choose, if there is no clarity of purpose in your life, she cannot be your helpmeet.

Wishing you all the best in your journey of self-discovery and fulfilment.

Warm Regards,

Keziah

THE YOUNG LADY

Dear Young Woman,

EMBRACE A PURPOSE-DRIVEN LIFE

I hope this letter finds you well. It is wonderful to hear that you are eager to live a purpose-driven life. This desire marks the beginning of a journey filled with fulfilment, growth and meaningful experiences. Here are some thoughts and advice to help you navigate this transformative path and make the most of your aspirations.

Define Your Purpose

1. **Identify Your Passions:** Reflect on what activities, courses or subjects ignite your enthusiasm. Understanding what excites you is the first step in uncovering your purpose.

2. **Clarify Your Values:** Take time to define your core values. These principles will guide your decisions and ensure that your actions align with what truly matters to you.

3. **Set Meaningful Goals:** Establish both short-term and long-term goals that resonate with your passions and values. Clear objectives provide direction and motivation. What life do you want to live and how are you going to make that happen?

Invest in Personal and Professional Growth

1. **Lifelong Learning:** Commit to continuous learning. Pursue education, attend workshops and seminars, read widely and stay curious.

Expanding your knowledge and skills is essential for personal and professional growth. There is so much information around us. Acquiring knowledge is easy in this dispensation if you are teachable. Do not just desire to acquire knowledge, apply the knowledge to your situation and become better.

2. **Develop Skills:** Focus on acquiring and honing skills that are relevant to your purpose. Practical skills enhance your ability to make a meaningful impact.

3. **Seek Mentorship:** Find mentors who can offer guidance, share their experiences and support your growth. Learning from others can provide valuable insights and accelerate your journey.

Cultivate Healthy Habits

1. **Physical Well-being:** Prioritize regular exercise, a balanced diet and sufficient sleep. A healthy body supports a vibrant mind and emotional resilience.

2. **Mental Health:** Practice mindfulness, meditation and stress management techniques. Taking care of your mental health is crucial for maintaining balance and focus.

3. **Consistency:** Establish routines that promote productivity and well-being. Consistent healthy habits lead to sustained positive changes.

Build Meaningful Relationships

1. **Positive Connections:** Surround yourself with people who inspire and uplift you. Positive relationships provide support and encouragement, fostering a nurturing environment.

2. **Effective Communication:** Develop strong communication skills. Effective communication builds understanding, trust and deeper connections in both personal and professional relationships.

3. **Supportive Community:** Engage in communities that share your interests and values. A supportive network can offer motivation and collaboration opportunities.

Practice Financial Responsibility

1. **Budget Wisely:** Create and adhere to a budget. Understanding your finances helps you make informed decisions and avoid unnecessary stress.

2. **Save and Invest:** Regularly save a portion of your income and consider investing for the future. Financial stability provides the freedom to pursue your purpose without undue worry.

3. **Live Within Your Means:** Avoid the temptation to live beyond your means. Financial discipline ensures long-term security and peace of mind. You cannot live a purpose-driven life when you spend all your money dressing to impress people who care less about your life.

Pursue Purpose with Passion

1. **Find Your Calling:** Identify activities and causes that resonate deeply with you. Pursuing your calling brings joy and fulfilment to your life.
2. **Make a Difference:** Seek ways to contribute positively to your community and the world. A purpose-driven life is enriched by the impact you make on others.
3. **Stay Authentic:** Follow your own path and make choices that align with your true self. Authenticity ensures that your purpose remains genuine and fulfilling.

Embrace Challenges and Learn from Failures

1. **Resilience:** Embrace challenges as opportunities for growth. Viewing setbacks as learning experiences strengthens your resilience.
2. **Adaptability:** Stay flexible and open to change. The ability to adapt is crucial in navigating life's uncertainties and seizing new opportunities.

3. **Perseverance:** Remain committed to your goals even when faced with obstacles. Perseverance is often the key to achieving a purpose-driven life.

Have you noticed that this is the same advice I gave to the young man? This should tell you that you are a full agentic adult too. Reconnect with yourself, own your life and live your dreams. Living a purpose-driven life is a noble and rewarding endeavour that requires dedication, self-awareness and consistent effort. By defining your purpose, investing in growth, cultivating healthy habits, building meaningful relationships, practicing financial responsibility, pursuing your passions and embracing challenges you can create a life filled with meaning and fulfilment.

Enjoy your journey towards a purpose-driven life. Embrace each step, learn from every experience and stay true to yourself.

With Warm Regards and Best Wishes For Your Journey.

Best Regards,

Keziah

Dear Young Lady,

EMBRACE YOUR FEMINITY AS A WOMAN

I hope this letter finds you well and filled with the radiance of your femininity. Today, I want to share some thoughts on the beauty of embracing your femininity, especially in the context of love and relationships. In a world that often celebrates qualities traditionally associated with masculinity, it is important to recognize and cherish the unique essence of being a woman.

Embracing Your Femininity

1. **Celebrate Your Strengths**: Your femininity is not a weakness; it is a source of immense strength and power. Embrace the qualities that make you uniquely feminine - your nurturing nature, emotional intelligence and intuitive wisdom. Celebrate these strengths and recognize the value they bring to your relationships and interactions with others.

2. **Trust Your Intuition**: As a woman, you possess a deep intuition that guides you in navigating life's complexities. Trust your instincts and listen to the wisdom of your inner voice. Your intuition can often lead you to make decisions that are in alignment with your true desires and values.

3. **Emotional Authenticity**: Allow yourself to express your emotions authentically and vulnerably.

Your ability to connect with and express your feelings is a beautiful aspect of your femininity. Embrace your emotional authenticity as a strength rather than a weakness and cultivate open and honest communication in your relationships.

Love and Femininity

1. **Receive Love Gracefully**: When you find a partner who loves and cares for you, allow yourself to receive his love gracefully. Embrace your femininity by allowing yourself to be cherished, nurtured and supported by your partner. Trust in his love and allow it to fill you with warmth and joy.

2. **Nurture Your Connection**: Cultivate a deep connection with your partner by embracing your feminine energy. Create moments of intimacy and tenderness that nourish your relationship and strengthen your bond. Your ability to nurture and care for your partner is a precious gift that enriches your connection.

3. **Balance and Harmony**: Embracing your femininity does not mean diminishing your partner's masculinity. Instead, strive for balance and harmony in your relationship where both partners can fully embrace and express your authentic selves.

Celebrate the unique qualities that each of you brings to the partnership, creating a dynamic and fulfilling union.

Self-Care and Empowerment

1. **Self-Care Rituals**: Prioritize self-care rituals that honour and nurture your femininity.

   Whether it is taking a relaxing bath, indulging in your favourite hobbies or spending time in nature. Make time for activities that replenish your spirit and rejuvenate your soul.

2. **Empowerment through Self-Love**: Practice self-love and self-compassion as acts of empowerment. Embrace your femininity wholeheartedly and celebrate the beauty of being a woman. When you love and honour yourself, you radiate confidence and authenticity, attracting love and respect from others.

3. **Support and Sisterhood**: Surround yourself with a supportive community of women who uplift and inspire you. Build sisterhood bonds based on mutual respect, empathy and empowerment. Together, you can celebrate your femininity and support each other in embracing your true selves.

As you journey through life and love, remember to embrace your femininity as a source of strength, beauty and authenticity. Trust in the power of your intuition, celebrate your emotional authenticity and nurture your connections with love and grace.

Embracing your femininity is not about conforming to societal expectations; it is about honouring the unique essence of who you are as a woman.

Wishing you a journey filled with love, joy and the radiant embrace of your femininity.

Warm Regards,

Keziah

Dear Young Lady,

BE MINDFUL OF HIS REALITY AND NOT HIS POTENTIAL

I hope this letter finds you well and thriving. As you navigate the exciting yet sometimes challenging world of relationships, let me share with you some insights that I believe are important to keep in mind. Specifically, I want to talk about the difference between a man's potential and his current reality and why it is crucial to focus on the latter when considering a long-term relationship.

Understanding Potential vs. Reality

1. **Potential is Future-Oriented**: Potential refers to what a person could become given the right circumstances, opportunities and efforts. It is about future possibilities and aspirations. While it is natural to be attracted to someone's potential, it is essential to recognize that potential is not necessarily a guarantee for the manifestation of a fulfilled future. Life is unpredictable and many factors can influence whether or not someone manifests his potential.

2. **Reality is Present-Oriented**: Reality, on the other hand, is about who the person is today. It encompasses their current habits, behaviours, values and life circumstances. When considering a long-term relationship, it is crucial to focus on this reality because it is what you will be living with day-to-day.

While people can grow and change, these changes often take time and are not always guaranteed.

Why Reality Matters

1. **Consistency and Reliability**: A person's current behaviour is a better predictor of their future actions than their potential. Look for consistency and reliability in how he handles responsibilities, treat others and manages his life. These qualities are essential for building a stable and trusting relationship.

2. **Shared Values and Compatibility**: Ensure that your values and life goals align with those of your partner, as they are now, not just what they aspire to be. Shared values and compatibility are crucial for a harmonious relationship. If there are significant differences in these areas, they are unlikely to change drastically in the future.

3. **Emotional and Financial Stability**: Assess the current emotional and financial stability of your partner. Emotional maturity and financial responsibility are foundational for a healthy relationship. Relying on the hope that these aspects will improve can lead to disappointment and strain in the relationship.

4. **Personal Growth**: While supporting each other's growth is important, it is crucial that both of you are independently committed to your personal development. Observe if your partner is actively working on bettering himself in the present rather than just talking

about future plans. There are many people in their sixties still talking about their future plans that they have not started working on yet.

Practical Tips

1. **Observe Actions Over Words**: Pay more attention to what your partner does rather than what they say they will do. Actions speak louder than words and are more indicative of their true character and priorities.

2. **Communicate Openly**: Have open and honest conversations about your expectations and future plans. Understand where your partner currently stands and his vision for the future with plans of implementing the vision. It is a plus if he has already started working on this dream. This will help you to ascertain if your paths are aligned and clearly note the role you can play in his vision.

3. **Set Boundaries and Standards**: Establish clear boundaries and standards for what you want and need in a relationship. Do not compromise on fundamental aspects hoping that things will improve over time. Your happiness and well-being should always come first.

4. **Seek Advice and Perspective**: Talk to trusted friends or mentors who know you well and can provide objective insights. Sometimes, those who are not emotionally involved can see things more clearly and offer valuable advice.

While it is wonderful to see and believe in someone's potential, it is their current reality that you will be living with every day. Being mindful of this reality helps ensure that you build a relationship based on mutual respect, shared values and present compatibility. This approach not only protects your emotional well-being but also sets the stage for a healthier and more fulfilling partnership.

Remember, you deserve to be with someone who adds value to your life as it is now and who complements your own journey of growth and self-discovery. Stay true to your values and do not settle for less than what you truly need and deserve in a partner.

Wishing you all the best in your journey to finding a loving and supportive relationship.

Warm Regards,

Keziah

Dear Young Lady,

INSTEAD OF LOOKING FOR A RICH MAN TO MARRY, WHY DON'T YOU MARRY AS A RICH WOMAN?

I hope this letter finds you in good health and high spirits. As you navigate the various facets of life and relationships, allow me to offer some thoughts on a topic that I believe is crucial to your independence and future happiness: financial freedom. It is important to focus on becoming financially free yourself rather than looking for a rich man to marry. Building your own financial independence Is empowering and offers a foundation for a more balanced and fulfilling life. There is a huge difference between money you will have to request and money you can manage and regulate yourself.

The Importance of Financial Independence

1. **Empowerment and Confidence**: Being financially independent gives you the confidence to make decisions that are best for you without relying on someone else's financial support. This empowerment allows you to pursue your dreams, take risks and live life on your terms.

2. **Security and Stability**: Financial freedom provides a sense of security and stability. Knowing that you can support yourself financially no matter what life throws your way reduces stress and anxiety. This security is invaluable and allows you to focus on other important aspects of life, such as personal growth and pursuing your passion.

3. **Equality in Relationships**: Entering a relationship as an equal partner rather than someone who is dependent on the other's wealth fosters mutual respect and balance. Financial independence ensures that you are with someone because you want to be not because you need to be. This balance is crucial for a healthy, respectful and loving relationship.

Steps to Achieve Financial Independence

1. **Education and Skills Development**: Invest in your education and continuously develop your skills. Knowledge and skills are powerful tools that can open doors to various opportunities and increase your earning potential. Whether it is pursuing higher education, acquiring certifications or learning new skills, investing in yourself pays off in the end. No educational system can teach you about being financially free; you will have to educate yourself.

2. **Career Planning**: Focus on building a career that aligns with your passions and strengths – a career you can passionately build. Set clear career goals and work diligently towards achieving them.

3. Seek mentorship, network with professionals in your field and always be on the lookout for opportunities to advance your career.

4. **Financial Literacy**: Educate yourself about personal finance. Understand the basics of budgeting, saving, investing and managing debt.

   Financial literacy empowers you to make informed decisions about your money and helps you build a solid financial foundation.

5. **Saving and Investing**: Develop a habit of saving a portion of your income regularly. Create an emergency fund to cover unexpected expenses. Additionally, learn about different investment options and start investing early. Investing helps grow your wealth over time and ensures long-term financial security. If you are single and yet you cannot save, surely you cannot save when you have a family.

6. **Avoiding Debt**: Be mindful of your spending habits and avoid accumulating unnecessary debt. Financial freedom is difficult to achieve if you are burdened with high-interest debt. Financial Freedom is not sexually transmitted, you will have to work towards it. Equally, understand that any money you did not work for will be difficult to regulate and manage because you may not have the capacity to do so.

7. **Setting Financial Goals**: Set short-term and long-term financial goals. Whether it is building a house, starting a business, saving for your children's education or planning for retirement, having clear goals helps you stay focused and motivated. Regularly review and adjust your goals as needed.

The Benefits of Financial Independence

1. **Personal Fulfilment**: Achieving financial independence brings a sense of personal fulfilment and pride.

   It reflects your hard work, determination and capability to take control of your life. This fulfilment is deeply satisfying and boosts your self-esteem.

2. **Freedom to Choose**: Financial independence gives you the freedom to make choices that align with your values and aspirations. You can choose the career you want, the lifestyle you desire and the relationships that truly enhance your life without being constrained by financial dependence.

3. **Balanced Relationships**: Relationships built on mutual respect, equity and equality are healthier and more sustainable. Financial independence ensures that you and your partner can support each other's growth and share responsibilities equally leading to a more balanced and fulfilling partnership.

While it is natural to appreciate financial stability in a partner, relying on someone else for financial security can lead to dependency and imbalance in a relationship. By focusing on achieving financial freedom yourself, not only do you empower yourself but you also set the stage for a healthier and equal relationship.

You have the ability to create a life of abundance and security through your own efforts and determination.

Embrace the journey of financial independence and you will find that it enhances every aspect of your life, including your well-being and relationships.

Wishing you all the best in your journey towards financial freedom and personal fulfilment.

Warm Regards,

Keziah

Dear Young Lady,

TO LIVE AN INTENTIONAL LIFE, YOU WILL HAVE TO BE MINDFUL OF THE COMPANY YOU KEEP

I hope this letter finds you well and in good spirits. As you continue to carve out your path in life, consider these thoughts on the importance of the friends and networks you keep. The people you surround yourself with have a profound impact on your personal and professional development. If you aim to lead a meaningful and fulfilling life, it is essential to be mindful of your relationships and the company you keep.

The Power of Positive Relationships

1. **Support and Encouragement**: Friends who genuinely care about your well-being will support and encourage you through life's vicissitudes. They will celebrate your successes and help you navigate challenges. Surround yourself with individuals who lift you up, inspire and motivate you to achieve your goals.

2. **Constructive Feedback**: Meaningful friends provide honest and constructive feedback. They help you see your blind spots, encourage self-improvement and hold you accountable. These friends are essential for your personal growth and development. Do not surround yourself with people who will tell you only what they know you will love to hear, the sycophants.

3. **Shared Values and Goals**: Building a network of friends who share your values and goals creates a sense of community and belonging. These connections reinforce your own beliefs and aspirations, making it easier to stay true to your path.

Building a Meaningful Network

1. **Quality over Quantity**: Focus on the quality of your friendships rather than the quantity. A few close and meaningful relationships are more valuable than a large number of superficial connections. Invest your time and energy in building deep, authentic relationships with people who genuinely care about you.

2. **Seek Like-Minded Individuals**: Join clubs, groups, organizations or communities that align with your interests and passions. Whether it is professional groups, hobby clubs or volunteer organizations, engaging with like-minded individuals can lead to meaningful connections and friendships.

3. **Diverse Perspectives**: While it is important to have friends with similar values, do not shy away from connecting with people who have different backgrounds and perspectives. Diverse friendships can broaden your horizons, challenge your thinking and enrich your life experiences.

4. **Mentorship and Guidance**: Seek out mentors who can provide guidance and support in your personal and professional journey. Mentors can offer valuable insights, share their experiences and help you navigate complex decisions. Building relationships with mentors can significantly enhance your growth and success.

Maintaining Healthy Relationships

1. **Mutual Respect and Trust**: Healthy relationships are built on mutual respect and trust. Ensure that your friendships are balanced and harmonious, where both parties give and receive – where you can pour into one other in various ways, respecting others boundaries and trustworthy in your actions and words.

2. **Open Communication**: Effective communication is key to maintaining strong relationships. Be open and honest with your friends about your thoughts, feelings and needs. Listen actively and empathetically to their perspectives as well. Clear and respectful communication fosters understanding and strengthens bonds.

3. **Support and Reciprocity**: Be there for your friends in times of need and celebrate their successes. Genuine support and reciprocity are the foundation of meaningful relationships. When you invest in your friends' well-being, you create a network of mutual support and care.

The friends and networks you cultivate play a crucial role in shaping your life. By surrounding yourself with positive, supportive and like-minded individuals, you create an environment that fosters personal growth, happiness and fulfilment. Be mindful of the relationships you invest in and prioritize those that add value to your life.

Remember, meaningful relationships are built on mutual respect, trust and support. Take the time to nurture these connections and you will find that they greatly enhance your journey towards a meaningful and fulfilling life.

Wishing you all the best in building and maintaining meaningful relationships.

Warm Regards,

Keziah

Dear Young Lady,

YOU CAN BE ASSERTIVE WITHOUT BEING ARROGANT

I hope this letter finds you well and thriving. Today, I want to engage your thoughts with a topic that is often misunderstood but incredibly important in both personal and professional settings: the difference between aggressiveness and assertiveness. As a woman navigating life's challenges and opportunities understanding this distinction can empower you to communicate effectively, set boundaries and assert yourself confidently.

Understanding Aggressiveness and Assertiveness

1. **Aggressiveness**: Aggressiveness is a communication style characterized by forcefulness, domination and disregard for others' feelings and boundaries. It often involves imposing one's will on others, using intimidation or manipulation to get what one wants. Aggressiveness can lead to conflict, resentment and strained relationships.

2. **Assertiveness**: Assertiveness on the other hand is a communication style that involves expressing your thoughts, feelings and needs in a clear, respectful and confident manner. It is about standing up for yourself while respecting the rights and boundaries of others. Assertiveness fosters open communication, mutual understanding and healthy relationships.

The Importance of Assertiveness

1. **Self-Advocacy**: Assertiveness empowers you to advocate for yourself and communicate your needs and desires effectively. It allows you to express your opinions, set boundaries and assert your rights without resorting to aggression or passivity. By being assertive, you emphasize your worth and value in any situation.

2. **Healthy Relationships**: Assertive communication fosters healthy, respectful and harmonious relationships. It encourages open dialogue, mutual respect and understanding between individuals. Assertive individuals are more likely to establish boundaries, resolve conflicts constructively and maintain positive connections with others.

3. **Confidence and Self-Esteem**: Assertiveness enhances your confidence and self-esteem. When you assert yourself confidently and respectfully, you reinforce your sense of self-worth and self-respect. This confidence radiates outward, positively influencing how others perceive and interact with you.

Practicing Assertiveness

1. **Clear Communication**: Clearly communicate your thoughts, feelings and needs using "I" statements. Express yourself in a direct, honest and respectful manner, avoiding passive or aggressive language. Be specific about what you want or need from others and listen actively to their responses.

2. **Setting Boundaries**: Establish and maintain healthy boundaries in your relationships. Clearly communicate your boundaries to others and assertively enforce them when necessary. Remember that it is okay to say no to requests or demands that conflict with your boundaries or values.

3. **Handling Conflict**: Approach conflict with a calm and assertive demeanour. Focus on addressing the issue at hand rather than attacking the person or people involved. Use active listening, empathy and problem-solving skills to find mutually beneficial solutions.

As you navigate life's challenges and interactions, remember that assertiveness is a valuable skill that can empower you to communicate effectively, set boundaries and assert your worth. By understanding the difference between aggressiveness and assertiveness and practicing assertive communication, you can cultivate healthy relationships, build confidence and live authentically.

Wishing you continued growth and empowerment on your journey.

Warm Regards,

Keziah

CHAPTER FOUR

THE MINISTRY OF THE PASTOR'S WIFE

Dear Pastor's Wife,

PRIORITISE YOUR EMOTIONAL WELL BEING AND SAFEGUARD YOUR MENTAL HEALTH

I hope this letter finds you in a moment of peace and reflection. As a supportive pillar behind the scenes of many congregations, you carry immense responsibilities and often find yourselves in the spotlight. On this occasion, I want you to digest my thoughts on aspects of your ministry that may often be overlooked - the importance of prioritizing your own emotional well-being and allowing yourself to heal from any wounds you may be carrying. As a psychosocial counsellor, a greater percentage of the clients I have worked with on mental health-related issues were pastors' wives. It is very pathetic to see many of you putting up the public façade of a successful life and ministry while inwardly you remain broken.

Acknowledging Emotional Wounds

1. **You're Human Too**: It is essential to recognize that you are human just like everyone else. Despite the expectations placed upon you, you are not immune to emotional pain or struggles. You may have experienced disappointments, hurts or traumas that have left deep wounds in your heart. You cannot be broken emotionally and try to maintain an aura of confidence and poise. All the unhealed traumas will manifest as autoimmune diseases.

Long lasting stress-related disorders, such as Post Traumatic Stress Disorder (PTSD) may increase your risk of autoimmune diseases.

PTSD may cause changes in your immune system that affect your hormone levels, stress response and inflammation. This may contribute to the development of autoimmune diseases.

I never understood what Karl Marx meant when he wrote, *"Religion is the opium of the masses,"* until I started working with many of your kind. Understand that your life can never go beyond your beliefs, paradigms and perspectives. Doing ministry is not about the accolade and reverence other people give to you; it is about the inner peace and satisfaction with which you do what you do even when there is no reward. Stop the people pleasing, find your niche and be your truest and authentic self.

To the wives of the General Overseers (GOs), owners and founders of churches, If other people decide to work with you, do not take them for granted and assume they have nothing else to do with their lives. They could serve God within their capacity anywhere and with anyone else. Accept them as full agentic adults; do not train them to be like you. Empower them to embrace their individuality and reward their contributions.

The Burden of Perfection: There is a common misconception that pastors' wives should always appear strong, composed and unshakeable. This pressure to maintain a flawless public facade can be exhausting and isolating. It is okay to admit when you are struggling and to seek support from others who are trustworthy. At a point, you will have to knuckle down to your *"hood"*, people you can share with who will not use your story as examples; people who are mature enough to know that certain issues or your information shared with them in confidence are for their ears only.

The Importance of Healing

1. **Permission to Heal**: Sometimes the people you work for and those you serve will not understand your personality and there will be clashes. People will mistreat you without apologising. People will judge you without listening to your side of the story. I remember a story of a pastor's wife who told her 'Mama GO' one day that, "If *all you hear about me, you can believe without even asking for my side of the story, then your covering over me is not enough."* People will intentionally discredit you to gain favours because many of these leaders see those who tell them lies about other people as the loyal ones – so sad but the reality. What is heart breaking is when the husband you are labouring with cannot protect you.

Some of your husbands can shout at you even at meetings with church members enabling the church members to disrespect you too under their watch.

Some pastors' wives have to attend different churches other than their husbands' to keep their sanity. Some pastors even take instructions from their GOs on how to treat their wives. If he being your husband and head is sold out to this *"opium"*, where is your place? Many of you are badly wounded, "broke *and broken*" yet you have been trained to normalise it. You are disrespected because you are poor - how can you not prioritise your own life yet expect to be financially free?

You have permission to prioritize your own healing journey. Acknowledge your emotional wounds, give yourself the time and space to process and heal from the wounds, hurts and demeaning acts. Healing is not a linear process and it is okay to seek professional help or support from professional counsellors not those who will use your stories to preach and make mockery of your pain.

Breaking the Cycle: By prioritizing your healing, you break the cycle of silent suffering and show others that it is okay not to be okay all the time. Your vulnerability and authenticity create a safe space for others to share their struggles and seek support without fear of judgment. Silence is not golden when you have something to say - something that affects your mental health.

Putting Away the Public Facade

1. **Authenticity and Vulnerability**: It is time to put away the public facade of being okay when you are dying inside. Embrace authenticity and vulnerability, both within yourself and within your communities. Share your struggles and triumphs openly, fostering deeper connections and understanding.

2. **Leading by Example**: As leaders within your communities, you have the opportunity to lead by example and demonstrate the power of vulnerability and authenticity. By showing that it is okay to be imperfect and vulnerable, you create a culture of compassion, empathy and support within your congregation.

Practicing Self-Care

1. **Prioritizing Self-Care**: Make self-care a priority in your life. Carve out time for activities that nourish your mind, body and soul, whether it is spending time in nature, visiting a spa, practicing mindfulness or engaging in creative pursuits. Remember that you cannot pour from an empty cup and taking good care of yourself is essential for your well-being.

2. **Seeking Support**: Do not hesitate to seek support from trusted friends or professionals when you need it. You do not have to carry your burdens alone.

There is strength in reaching out for help when you need it most. Research indicates that seeking help early saves one from unnecessary stress related to the difficulty.

Dear pastors wives, you are valued, cherished and worthy of love and support. Allow yourselves to heal from any emotional wounds you may be carrying and put away the public facade of being okay when you are struggling inside. Embrace authenticity, vulnerability and self-care as essential components of your journey toward healing and wholeness.

You are not alone there is a community of support waiting to uplift and empower you. May you find solace in the journey of healing and emerge stronger, more resilient and more authentically yourself than ever before.

With Love and Solidarity,

Keziah

Dear Pastor's Wife,

THERE IS A HUGE DIFFERENCE BETWEEN CHURCH ACTIVITIES AND A RELATIONSHIP WITH GOD

I hope this letter finds you in good health and spirits. I take this moment to bring to the fore some thoughts regarding an important topic that I believe is crucial for all believers to understand – the difference between church activities and a relationship with God.

I want to encourage you to distinguish between engaging in church activities and nurturing your personal relationship with God. It is essential to prioritize cultivating a deep and personal connection with the Lord over merely participating in routine church functions. Your spiritual growth and well-being greatly depend on investing time and effort into building an intimate and authentic relationship with God. While church activities are valuable, they should never replace or overshadow the sacred bond you have with the Lord. Remember to seek His presence, guidance and wisdom in all that you do, allowing your relationship with him to be the cornerstone of your life and ministry.

Firstly, let me express my gratitude for your unwavering dedication and commitment to the church. Your tireless efforts in organising and participating in various activities are truly commendable.

These activities play a vital role in nurturing the spiritual growth of the congregation and fostering a sense of community among the members.

However, it is important to remember that church activities, no matter how significant are not an end in themselves. They are meant to serve as vehicles through which we can deepen our relationship with God. It is all too easy to get caught up in the busyness of church life and lose sight of the true purpose behind your actions. A relationship with God is a deeply personal and intimate connection that goes beyond attendance at church services or involvement in ministry events. It is a daily walk, a constant pursuit of his presence and a surrendering of your life to his will. It requires you to cultivate a genuine love for God to seek him in prayer and meditation and to study his word diligently.

While church activities can certainly facilitate your spiritual growth, they should never replace or overshadow your individual relationship with God. It is essential to prioritize your personal time with him, allowing him to speak in your heart, guide your steps and transform you from within. This intimate communion with God is what sustains you during challenging times, strengthens your faith and empowers you to serve others effectively.

As a pastor's wife, you have a unique opportunity to lead by example and encourage others to seek a deeper relationship with God. Increase your capacity in order to be an asset to your husband and the ministry.

Share your own experience of encountering his presence, emphasize the importance of personal devotion and provide guidance on how to develop spiritual disciplines. Remember, church activities are means to an end and that end is a vibrant and thriving relationship with your heavenly Father. Always strive to keep this truth at the forefront of your mind and heart, both in your own life and as you minster to others. May God continue to bless and guide you to navigate accurately, the balance between church activities and nurturing a personal relationship with him.

With Much Love and Blessings,

Keziah

Dear Pastor's Wife,

BE CAREFUL OF MENTORS WHO ARE TORMENTORS

I hope this letter finds you well. As you navigate your important role within the church community, reflect on these thoughts that can significantly influence your well-being and leadership: the choice of mentors.

Having mentors can be incredibly valuable; offering guidance, support and wisdom as you fulfil your responsibilities. However, it is crucial to differentiate between mentors who genuinely support and nurture your growth and those who may intentionally or unintentionally act as tormentors, stifling your authenticity and well-being. Here are some points to consider to ensure you align yourself with positive and uplifting mentorship. If you will have to dim your light so your light does not shine brighter because it makes your mentor uncomfortable, know that you are with the wrong mentor. Choose the right mentors for authentic leadership.

Recognize Authentic Mentorship

1. **Supportive Guidance:** A true mentor provides supportive and constructive guidance. They celebrate your successes, help you navigate challenges and encourage your personal and spiritual growth.

2. **Mutual Respect:** Authentic mentors respect your individuality and leadership style. They offer advice and wisdom without imposing their own agenda on you or diminishing your unique contributions. A genuine mentor respects you and commands your respect too.

3. **Empowerment:** The right mentor empowers you to make your own decisions and fosters confidence in your abilities. They believe in your potential and encourage you to pursue your vision unless otherwise they are using you to service their legacy.

Identifying Tormenting Influences

1. **Manipulation and Control:** Be cautious of mentors who seek to manipulate or control your actions and decisions. Leadership under such influence can lead to a loss of your authentic voice and vision.

2. **Unconstructive Criticism:** Mentors who consistently criticize without providing constructive feedback can erode your self-esteem and hinder your growth. Constructive feedback is essential but it should always aim to build you up not tear you down.

3. **Disrespect and Undermining:** If a mentor frequently disrespects your opinions, undermines your efforts or belittles your achievements, it is a clear sign of a toxic influence.

Such behaviour can cause significant emotional distress and impede your effectiveness as a leader.

Choosing the Right Mentors

1. **Shared Values:** Seek mentors whose values align with yours and who genuinely understand and respect your role as a pastor's wife. Shared values create a foundation of trust and mutual understanding.
2. **Positive Track Record:** Look for mentors with a proven record of accomplishment of positive influence and successful leadership. Their experience and wisdom can be invaluable for your own journey.
3. **Personal Connection:** A mentor-mentee relationship should have a strong personal connection. You should feel comfortable sharing your thoughts, challenges and aspirations with them without fear of unfounded judgment.

Maintaining Your Authenticity

1. **Self-Reflection:** Regularly engage in self-reflection to stay connected with your core values, beliefs and leadership style. This practice will help you maintain your authenticity even in challenging situations.

2. **Set Boundaries:** Establish clear boundaries to protect your emotional and mental well-being. It is okay to distance yourself from mentors who do not support your authentic self.

3. **Seek Diverse Perspectives:** While having a primary mentor is valuable, seeking advice from a diverse group of supportive individuals can provide a broader perspective and enrich your leadership approach. Only narcissistic mentors will teach you not to value anyone else but them.

Your role as a pastor's wife is both challenging and rewarding. Having the right mentors can make a significant difference in your journey. By carefully choosing mentors who uplift and empower you and avoiding those who act as tormentors - those who act as if they are your mediators and without them you cannot reach out to God, you can play your role very well and find fulfilment as well. Be careful of those who claim without their covering, your life is over – that is demonic. You will need to find God for yourself and connect to him directly so you can lead authentically and effectively.

Remember, your voice and vision are important and the right mentors will always encourage you to shine in your unique way.

With Warm Regards and Best Wishes,

Keziah

CHAPTER FIVE

LETTERS TO DADDY G.Os, MAMA G.Os AND PASTORS WORKING FOR OTHERS

Dear Religious Leaders and Your Esteemed Wives,

BE THE EMPLOYER THAT YOU ARE SUPPOSED TO BE UNTO THOSE WHO WORK FOR YOU

I hope this letter finds you well. As you continue to uphold the values of your faith and nurture the spiritual growth of your community, it is crucial that you take a moment to reflect on the contributions of those who dedicate their lives to supporting your mission and building your legacy.

Our churches are not merely buildings; they are vibrant communities of believers who rely on the dedication and hard work of many individuals behind the scenes. From the faithful volunteer pastors (volunteers because you don't pay them salary) who tirelessly serve in various ministries to the staff members who manage daily operations with unwavering commitment, each person plays a pivotal role in shaping the present and future of your organisation.

It is therefore incumbent on you as owners to ensure that these individuals are not only recognized but also appreciated for their efforts. Just the same way you view the church as any other organisation that is supposed to yield profits and grow – the people that make these happen are to be catered for as any serious organisation will do. Excellence in productivity and excellence in the welfare and well-being of the workers too.

Too often, their sacrifices go unnoticed or underappreciated. Their commitment deserves more than mere acknowledgments; it warrants genuine gratitude and meaningful recognitions. Without the efforts and sacrifices of these people, there will be no legacies for you. How could you not care about their welfare? Do you know they could have used the same efforts, time and contribution to build for themselves too?

I encourage each of you to take proactive steps to foster a culture of appreciation within your church community:

1. **Recognition Programs:** Establish formal mechanisms to publicly acknowledge the contributions of the people who sacrificed their lives to build your ministries. They could have built with the same efforts for themselves. Show them respect. Some of you respect even your younger biological children than your pastors who have devoted their time and efforts to build your empire. That is pathetic.

2. **A Workman Deserves His WAGES:** Take the time to personally express gratitude to individuals who go above and beyond their duties. Do not wait for your pastors to have serious medical conditions or die before you support them or give them a befitting burial - that is counterproductive and hypocritical. If they are your employees, then be the employer that you are supposed to be unto them.

Do not be like the worldly leaders who are concerned only about those who can give them fat envelopes and expensive gifts. If after they have used their time, efforts, gifts and talents to build your legacy, they are to show you honour by periodically bestowing material things upon you to show their allegiance and loyalty, then it seems they are in a cult but not serving in a church. Honour is not a levy or a task and loyalty is not a one-way street. The fat envelopes and expensive gifts have caused many of you to miss the real loyal ones.

3. **Support and Care:** Ensure that those who dedicate their lives to serve your vision feel supported and valued not only for their work but also as individuals. Offer support and assistance to those who perpetuate your vision rather than the public show of love and affection you give to strangers in the eye of the public. It does not matter how you manipulate these pastors into believing the vision is for them too – you know that is not the case and the God you serve equally knows that is not the case.

4. **Feedback and Listening:** Actively seek feedback from your volunteers and staff to understand their needs and concerns. Do not let all your trainings be on how they can generate more money from their congregants, build ultra-modern infrastructures and gain more members to the church.

Create an environment where they feel comfortable sharing their thoughts and ideas relating to their welfare and wellbeing.

By prioritizing the well-being and recognition of those who contribute to your ministries, you not only strengthen your community but also demonstrate the love and appreciation that lie at the heart of your faith. Emotional sentiments are not compassion - get proper systems and structures that see to the welfare and well-being of your pastors and workers.

Thank you for your attention to this important matter. Let your focus be to build a ministry where all pastors, their spouses and your church workers are valued, respected and cherished for their unique gifts and contributions. The God who called you cherishes these.

With Warm Regards,

Keziah

Dear Pastors,

ENCOURAGEMENT TO PURSUE ADDITIONAL

INCOME STREAMS

I hope this letter finds you in good health and high spirits. As spiritual leaders, your dedication and service to our communities are deeply valued and appreciated. However, I am writing to address a concern that affects many of you: financial stability. You can be highly anointed yet *'broke and broken'*. You will need foresight and insight into how to generate additional source of income aside your salary or allowance as a pastor. Do you have a skill set that you can monetise?

It is widely acknowledged that pastors are among those who are poorly paid – especially those who do not have their own churches – those who work for others. Whilst many of those who own these churches live in homes like seven-star hotels, majority of you who are working for them are struggling to pay even your house rents. This situation can create undue stress and distract you from the important work you do; guiding and nurturing your congregations. It is important to understand that these financial constraints are not a reflection of the value placed on your ministry. Unless you want to go the way of your colleagues who are manipulating, exploiting and extorting money from their congregants – your financial freedom is your responsibility not the churches'.

Let your desire be to make impact, be relevant and out of your relevance, you will attract money.

You can pastor a church and still be a successful entrepreneur or have a good paying job. If you are taking home money from any employer that cannot take you home, you will need to have a conversation with yourself. That means you need a better or another source of income. Your time is your life so consider how you are using your time. Anything that wastes your time is equally wasting your life.

In light of this, I strongly encourage you to consider pursuing additional income streams or *"side hustles"* that can supplement your church's salary/allowance. Engaging in other forms of work can provide you with the financial security needed to support your family and personal goals, while also allowing you to continue your vital ministry work without undue financial pressure. I hope you fully understand that somethings are prayed for but many other things are paid for. Develop and deploy your gifts and talents and positively monetise them. Find your niche, Man of God.

Here are a few suggestions to consider:

1. **Leveraging Your Skills:** Identify skills or talents you have that can be monetised. This could include writing, teaching, professional counselling or even creative arts.

Online platforms offer numerous opportunities to reach a wider audience.

2. **Consulting and Coaching:** Offer your expertise in leadership, counselling or spiritual guidance to other organizations or individuals on a consulting basis. Many people and organizations seek out experienced leaders for mentorship and advice.

3. **Investments:** Consider learning about financial freedom and investing in financial markets or real estate. While this requires some initial knowledge and capital, it can provide a passive income over time.

4. **Part-Time Work:** Explore part-time job opportunities that are flexible enough to fit around your pastoral duties. This could include teaching at a local school or university, freelance work or even starting a business.

5. **Online Platforms:** Utilize online platforms to teach, write or preach that can generate income. Websites like YouTube and Facebook pay depending on how you grow your channel or page.   Personal blogs can provide a source of revenue through ad income, subscriptions and donations.

6. **Entrepreneurship:** If you have a passion for a particular product or service, consider starting a business. This could be anything from farming, a bookshop, internet café, starting a school or even an online store.

It is important to choose ventures that align with your values and passions, ensuring that they complement your pastoral duties rather than detract from them.

Balancing additional work with your responsibilities as a pastor will require careful time management and prioritization but it can be done successfully with proper planning. Some of you claim the God that called you will take care of you so you do not need to do any work apart from your pastoral duties, yet the manner in which you exploit and manipulate your church members to give so your needs can be met is disgraceful to the God that called you. You cannot depend on people's gifts to live your life; there are no guarantees with that.

By diversifying your income sources, you can achieve greater financial stability and peace of mind, allowing you to focus more fully on your ministry and the spiritual well-being of your congregation.

Thank you for your dedication and hard work. May God continue to bless you and guide you in all your endeavours.

With Warm Regards and Blessings,

Keziah

Dear Pastors,

HONOUR GOD IN YOUR PRIVATE LIVES AND RECOGNIZE THE CONTRIBUTIONS OF YOUR WIVES IN MINISTRY

I hope this letter finds you well. As spiritual leaders dedicated to guiding your congregations and spreading the message of your faith, your commitment and devotion to the cause are truly commendable. Today, I want to emphasize a crucial aspect of ministry success that is often overlooked: the importance of honouring God in your private lives and recognizing the invaluable contributions of your wives.

In 1 Peter 3:7, it is written: *"Husbands, in the same way be considerate as you live with your wives, and treat them with respect as the weaker partner and as heirs with you of the gracious gift of life, so that nothing will hinder your prayers."* This scripture highlights the importance of treating your wives with honour and respect, acknowledging their role as equal partners in the gracious gift of life.

Your private life, away from the pulpit, is where the true test of your character and faith lies. The way you conduct yourself in private, particularly in your relationships with your family, directly influences your ministry. Here are a few key points to consider:

1. **Integrity in Private Life:** Your actions and decisions behind closed doors are as important, if not more so, than your public persona. Strive to lead a life of integrity, humility and faithfulness. Your private worship, prayer life and devotion to God set the foundation for your public ministry.

2. **Honouring Your Wife:** Your wife is a vital partner in your ministry. Her support, encouragement and sacrifices often go unrecognized yet they are essential to your success. Show her respect, appreciation and love. Acknowledge her contributions publicly and privately, ensuring she knows how valued and important she is to both you and your ministry. Show me a pastor who is successful in ministry and I will point to you a servant of God who honours God and honours his wife.

3. **Shared Ministry Vision:** Work together with your wife to create a shared vision for your ministry. Her insights and perspectives can provide invaluable guidance and balance. Involve her in decision-making processes and seek her counsel regularly.

4. **Balance and Prioritization:** Maintain a healthy balance between your ministry and family life. Prioritize your relationship with your wife and children, ensuring they receive

the time and attention they deserve. A strong, united family is a powerful testimony to your congregation.

5. **Prayer and Spiritual Growth:** Pray together as a couple and seek spiritual growth jointly. Encourage each other in your faith journeys and support each another in your individual callings. A united spiritual front will fortify your ministry and personal life.

6. **Role Modelling:** Your relationship with your wife serves as a model for your congregation. Demonstrating love, respect and partnership in your marriage sets a powerful example for others to follow. It shows that honouring God starts at home and extends to all aspects of life.

By honouring God in your private life and recognizing the contributions of your wife, not only do you strengthen your personal relationships but also enhance the effectiveness of your ministry. Your congregation will see the authenticity of your faith and be inspired by the example you set.

Thank you for your dedication and service. May God continue to bless you, your family and your ministry as you strive to honour Him in all aspects of your life.

With Warm Regards and Blessings,

Keziah

CHAPTER SIX

LETTERS TO THOSE ON THE FIFTH FLOOR AND BEYOND

YOU CAN BE HEALTHIER AND HAPPIER

AFTER 50

Dear Friends,

YOU CANNOT BE BITTER AND BETTER SIMULTANEOUSLY. WHY WILL YOU CHOOSE TO BE BITTER?

As a psychosocial counsellor working with people in their 50s and beyond, though I am now climbing the fifth floor, I have so much to share. Reaching your 50s brings a wealth of experience and wisdom but it can also come with its share of disappointments and difficulties. It is easy to let past grievances and setbacks lead to bitterness. However, embracing a mindset focused on personal growth and improvement - being better instead of being bitter can lead to a more fulfilling and joyful life. Here are some thoughts and advice on how to cultivate this positive approach.

People can become bitter instead of bettering their situation for variety of reasons. Sometimes, individuals may feel overwhelmed by their circumstances and struggles so much that they cannot see any way to improve. They may also have experienced repeated setbacks or disappointments that have led to feelings of resentment and pessimism. Factors such as lack of support, resources or opportunities can contribute to a sense of hopelessness. It is important to recognize that each person's experience is unique. Therefore, addressing bitterness will often require empathy, understanding and support.

Reasons for bitterness

Some people think and believe they have worked so hard with fewer results to show for their efforts. For example, someone who studied hard and got good grades but could not get a good job might be bitter. Someone who gave up the fun stuff of life for a promised reward that never materialized could be bitter too. Someone who invested so much in others, hoping and believing that these people will come to their aid when they need them one day and yet they were abandoned and neglected when in need could be bitter.

Emotional wounds: People who have experienced significant emotional pain, such as betrayal, rejection or trauma may find it difficult to move forward and may develop a bitter outlook as a defence mechanism. The bitterness can act as a shield to protect them from further hurt or disappointment.

Learned helplessness: When individuals repeatedly face obstacles or challenges without perceiving any control or ability to change their circumstances, they may develop a sense of learned helplessness. They cement the belief that their actions cannot make a difference and this can lead to feelings of bitterness and resignation in their 'assumed fate'.

Lack of support: A lack of support from family, friends or the community can make it harder for individuals to improve their situation. Without encouragement, guidance or resources, they may struggle to see a path towards betterment and may become bitter as a result.

Cognitive biases: Our cognitive biases can influence how we perceive and interpret events. For example, confirmation bias leads us to seek out information that confirms our existing beliefs, which can reinforce negative attitudes and prevent us from seeing opportunities for improvement. Other biases like pessimism bias or attribution bias, can also contribute to a bitter mindset. In such scenarios, the victim will not even believe something good could come out of his/her life.

Lack of self-awareness: Some people may struggle with self-reflection and fail to recognize their own role in their circumstances. They may blame external factors or other people for their problems. This can prevent them from taking responsibility and actively working towards bettering their situation. You can only own your life when you accept that you are in charge and therefore responsible for your wins and losses.

Loss of hope: When individuals face prolonged or repeated adversity without seeing any signs of improvement, they may lose hope for a better future.

This loss of hope can lead to bitterness as they may feel that their efforts are futile or that life is inherently unfair.

Lack of coping skills: Some individuals may lack effective coping skills to deal with challenges and setbacks. Without healthy strategies to manage stress and navigate difficulties, they may become overwhelmed and develop a bitter outlook as a way to cope with their emotions.

Negative influences: Negative influences from peers, family members or the media can also contribute to bitterness. When individuals are surrounded by people who reinforce negative beliefs or engage in destructive behaviours, it can be challenging for them to break free from a bitter mindset and work towards bettering their situation.

Lack of self-worth: Low self-esteem or feelings of inadequacy can hinder individuals from taking steps to improve their situation. They may believe they are unworthy of positive change or that they do not deserve better. Such a situation may lead to bitterness and self-sabotaging behaviours.

Resistance to vulnerability: Moving towards a better situation often requires individuals to be vulnerable, take risks and ask for help. Some people may resist vulnerability due to fear of rejection, judgment or further disappointment.

This resistance can keep them stuck in bitterness and prevent them from seeking the support they need.

Lack of awareness or options: People may remain bitter because they are unaware of the available resources, opportunities or alternative paths that could lead to improvement. Limited exposure or access to information can hinder their ability to make informed decisions and take proactive steps to overcome bitterness.

It is important to note that overcoming bitterness is a complex and individual process. It often involves a combination of self-reflection, emotional healing, building resilience, seeking support and taking action towards positive change. Professional guidance, such as therapy or coaching, can be invaluable in helping individuals address bitterness and work towards bettering their situation.

While bitterness can be a natural response to challenging circumstances, it is not a productive or healthy long-term state. Encouraging empathy, providing support, promoting self-reflection and offering opportunities for growth and empowerment can help individuals shift from bitterness to a more positive and proactive mindset.

Developing effective coping skills to navigate challenges and setbacks is essential for personal growth and resilience. Here are some strategies individuals can employ:

- **Self-awareness**: Start by developing self-awareness and understanding your own emotional and behavioural patterns. Pay attention to how you react to challenges and setbacks. Identify any negative or unhelpful coping mechanisms you tend to rely on, such as avoidance, self-blame or destructive behaviours.

- **Identify triggers**: Identify the specific situations, events or thoughts that trigger stress, anxiety or negative emotions for you. Understanding your triggers can help you anticipate and prepare for challenges, allowing you to implement appropriate coping strategies in advance.

- **Seek support**: Reach out to trustworthy and supportive friends, family members or professionals such as therapists or counsellors. Talking openly about your challenges and setbacks can provide emotional validation, different perspectives and practical advice. Supportive relationships can also provide a sense of belonging and encouragement during difficult times.

- **Develop healthy coping mechanisms**: Explore and practice healthy coping mechanisms that work for you. Examples include engaging in regular physical exercise, practicing mindfulness or meditation, journaling, engaging in hobbies or creative outlets, seeking social support and using relaxation techniques such as deep breathing or progressive muscle relaxation. Experiment with different strategies to find what resonates with you and brings you relief.

- **Challenge negative thinking**: Develop skills to challenge and reframe negative thinking patterns. Practice identifying and replacing negative or self-defeating thoughts with more positive and realistic ones. This can help you develop a more optimistic and resilient mindset.

- **Set realistic goals**: Break down larger challenges into smaller, manageable goals. Setting realistic and achievable goals can provide a sense of direction and progress. Celebrate small victories along the way to maintain motivation and build confidence.

- **Practice self-care**: Prioritize self-care and make time for activities that rejuvenate and nourish you. This can include getting enough sleep, maintaining a balanced diet, engaging in activities you enjoy, spending time in nature and practicing relaxation techniques.

- **Learn from setbacks**: Instead of dwelling on setbacks, view them as learning opportunities. Reflect on what you can learn from the experience and how you can use it to grow and improve. Adopting a growth mindset can help you see setbacks as temporary and part of the learning process.

- **Build resilience**: Resilience is the ability to bounce back from adversity. Cultivate resilience by developing a strong support network, cultivating a positive and optimistic mindset, practicing gratitude, embracing change and uncertainty and fostering adaptability.

- **Seek professional help when needed**: When you find it challenging to develop effective coping skills or if your challenges and setbacks are significantly affecting your well-being, consider seeking professional help. Therapists, counsellors or coaches can provide guidance, support and specific coping strategies tailored to your needs.

Remember that developing effective coping skills takes time and practice. Be patient with yourself and be open to trying different strategies until you find what works best for you.

How can individuals develop effective coping skills to navigate challenges and setbacks?

Having something happen to you that caused major disappointment and loss can make a person feel bitter. If that person was the victim of another, they may find themselves unable to recover and move on with their lives. It is more than a grudge or regret. There is anger and hatred toward the perpetrator as well as themselves for wrongly trusting. It is very hard to overcome those feelings of bitterness toward a situation or a person you feel did you dirty. I have been in those shoes and understand those yucky feelings. I know you remember the sleepless nights and anxiety. The moments you wanted justice! However, justice never came and you had to live with the pain and try to recover from the damage done.

You thought how could someone you loved or trusted do such a thing to you and live with himself or herself?

In your anger, some of you even wished them bad and Karma to find them. Some of you have prayed to God to take that hatred from your heart. Unfortunately, it changed your perception of life and trust toward others. You try to be more cautious of the wolves in sheep's clothing. *"Long gone are the days of innocence,"* became your slogan. You look at the world and others with caution and fear of getting hurt. That sweet and loving nature of yours is still there, but not for all to see or use.

Bitterness not only causes symptoms of trauma like sleeplessness, fatigue and lack of libido. It can also in the long-term lead to low self-confidence, negative personality shifts and an inability to have a healthy relationship. It is not worth it, my darling. I want to be happier and healthier after sixty and beyond, I cannot habour emotions and sentiments that destroy me whilst the person who hurt me is enjoying his or her life.

Resentment and bitterness are powerful emotions that can consume us from the inside out. While most of us are aware of their negative impact on our mental well-being, we often overlook their physical consequences. Let us explore the often-underestimated physical dangers of holding on to resentment and bitterness.

Understanding these risks can motivate us to let go and move towards healthier emotions and perspectives.

1. Elevated Blood Pressure

Resentment and bitterness can raise your blood pressure, which is a significant risk factor for heart disease and stroke. When you are in a state of emotional turmoil, your body goes into fight-or-flight mode, causing your heart to pump harder and faster than usual. Over time, this extra strain on your cardiovascular system can contribute to hypertension, a condition that can have serious long-term health consequences.

2. Weakened Immune System

The link between emotions and the immune system is well established. Research has shown that chronic bitterness and resentment can weaken your body's ability to fight off infections and illnesses. This is because the persistent release of stress hormones suppresses the immune system's functions. You therefore become more susceptible to infections and it takes a longer period for your body to recover when you are indisposed.

3. Increased Stress Levels

Resentment and bitterness are like toxic fuel for stress. When you harbour these negative emotions, your body's stress response is continually activated, releasing stress hormones like cortisol and adrenaline into your bloodstream. This constant state of stress can lead to a host of physical issues including high blood pressure, increased heart rate and a weakened immune system.

Over time, chronic stress can contribute to serious conditions such as cardiovascular disease and autoimmune disorders.

4. Insomnia and Sleep Disorders

Emotions like resentment and bitterness can wreak havoc on your sleep patterns. When you are consumed by negative feelings, your mind races, making it difficult to relax and fall asleep. Even when you do manage to drift off, you are more likely to experience disrupted sleep and waking up throughout the night. Chronic sleep deprivation is associated with a multitude of health problems, including obesity, diabetes and cognitive impairment.

5. Digestive Issues

Your gut is often called your *"second brain"* because of its close connection to your emotional well-being. Holding on to resentment and bitterness can disrupt the delicate balance of your digestive system. Stress-induced changes in gut function can lead to gastrointestinal problems like irritable bowel syndrome (IBS), indigestion and acid reflux. Additionally, emotional distress can alter your eating habits, potentially leading to overeating or undereating, both of which can have negative consequences on your digestive health.

6. Muscle Tension and Pain

Emotional tension can manifest physically in the form of muscle stiffness and pain. When you are filled with resentment and bitterness, you may unconsciously tense your muscles, particularly in your neck, shoulders and back. This chronic muscle tension can lead to discomfort, headaches and even chronic pain conditions. Over time, it can severely affect your mobility and overall quality of life.

7. Accelerated Aging

Possibly one of the most surprising physical dangers of resentment and bitterness is their potential to accelerate the aging process. Chronic stress, driven by these negative emotions can lead to premature aging of the skin, making you appear older than your actual age. Additionally, stress-induced inflammation has been linked to cellular aging and shortened telomeres, which are protective caps on your DNA strands. Shortened telomeres are associated with a higher risk of age-related diseases like cancer and dementia.

While it is natural to experience resentment and bitterness at times, it is essential to recognize their physical dangers. These emotions if left unchecked, can wreak havoc on your body, leading to stress-related health problems, weakened immunity, digestive issues, sleep disturbances, muscle tension and even accelerated aging.

Understanding the physical consequences of holding on to these emotions can be a powerful motivator to let go and seek healthier ways to cope with negative feelings. By practicing forgiveness, empathy and self-care, you can protect both your mental and physical well-being, leading to a happier and healthier life. You can put on the public façade of a successful life but you cannot deceive your soul.

The success, fame and accolades might look like you have it all together, succeeding on a higher level on the outside yet you are depressed because of bitterness. Someone might never understand why another person with these levels of success, things like a great career, a perfect marriage and family dynamics should struggle so much internally.

The truth is no exterior thing can heal your traumas. Healing is a journey that comprises ego death. A bad day for the ego is a great day for the soul, they say. People are always going to be fickle. It is all about how you feel about yourself.

People are always going to be people; they will love you today and discard you tomorrow, appreciate your services today and find you useless tomorrow; good people do bad things, bad things happen to good people, we do bad things to ourselves too. Our poor choices, being afraid to take the needed risks, being irresponsible, allowing others to treat us poorly in the name of whatever. Through all of these, we march on regardless.

The unresolved emotions; unaddressed pain; anger or resentment can fester and turn into bitterness. That negative mindset, a pessimistic outlook can lead to a cycle of bitterness as you focus on the negative aspects of life.

The unmet expectations, when reality does not meet our expectations, disappointment can turn into bitterness. As we age, some become disillusioned with the present and nostalgic for the past, leading to bitterness. To many others too, it is the lack of purpose or meaning in life; feeling unfulfilled or without a sense of direction can lead to bitterness and discontent. If you find yourself in this situation, ask yourself the following questions and sincerely answer yourself.

1. Who am I?
2. Where am I with my life right now?
3. Where do I need to be?
4. How do I bridge the gap between where I am now and where I need to be?

No one is guaranteed tomorrow, why are you wasting today because of yesterday's pain? Remember, bitterness is not a fixed state - it is possible to recognize and work on overcoming it, allowing ourselves to grow and become better versions of ourselves.

The power to shape your outlook and experience lies within you. I came across a saying that resonated very well with me, the author unknown.

"In life, you will fall out with people you never thought you would. You will get betrayed by people you trusted with all your heart and get used by people you would do anything for. Nevertheless, life also has a beautiful side to it. You will get loved by people you never thought you would have, form new friendships with people that will establish more meaningful and stronger relationships, overcome things you never thought you would get over. We all have chapters that end with people at some point in life. Take pride in knowing that the very best part of your book is still being written."

Here is to a future filled with growth, positivity and fulfilment.

With Warm Regards and Best Wishes,

Keziah

Dear Friends,

EMBRACE YOUR 50S:
THE PATH TO HEALTHIER AND HAPPIER YEARS AHEAD

As we step into our 50s, it is natural to reflect on our past and ponder what lies ahead. While society often places undue emphasis on the youth, the truth is that this decade can be one of the healthiest and happiest periods of our lives. With a mindful approach, the wisdom gained over the years and a few strategic lifestyle adjustments, we can thrive in ways we never imagined possible.

Prioritize Your Physical Health

1. **Regular Exercise:** Incorporating regular physical activity is crucial. Whether it is brisk walking, swimming, yoga or strength training, find an activity you enjoy. Exercise not only maintains physical health but also boosts mental well-being.

   Balanced Diet: A nutritious diet rich in fruits, vegetables, lean proteins and whole grains is essential. Consider consulting a nutritionist to tailor a diet that suits your specific needs and supports your overall health.

2. **Routine Check-ups:** Regular medical check-ups and screenings can catch potential health issues early. Staying on top of your health means fewer surprises and more time of living purposefully and intentionally.

Mental and Emotional Well-being

1. **Mindfulness and Relaxation:** Practices like meditation, deep breathing exercises or simply spending time in nature can significantly reduce stress. Mindfulness helps keep us present and appreciative of the moment.

2. **Social Connections:** Maintain and nurture relationships with family, friends and community. Social interactions are key to emotional health and provide a support system that enriches life.

3. **Pursue Passions:** Engaging in hobbies and activities that bring you joy can provide a sense of purpose and fulfilment. Whether it is livestock farming, painting, gardening, traveling or learning something new, now is the perfect time to invest in what you love.

Lifelong Learning and Growth

1. **New Skills and Knowledge:** Embrace learning new things, whether it is a new language, musical instrument or a professional skill. Keeping the mind active and engaged can be incredibly rewarding and staves off cognitive decline.

2. **Goal Setting:** Set new personal and professional goals. Achieving these goals, no matter how small can boost self-esteem and provide a sense of accomplishment. *"You are never too old to set another goal or to dream a new dream".* C. S. Lewis. The KFC founder said, *"Just because you took longer than others doesn't mean you failed. I started KFC at 65." "There is a powerful driving force inside every human being that, once unleashed can make any vision, dream or desire a reality."* Tony Robbins.

Positive Mindset and Attitude

1. **Practice Gratitude:** Regularly reflecting on what you are thankful for can improve your outlook on life. A positive mindset can make a significant difference in your overall happiness.

2. **Adaptability:** Life will continue to change, being flexible and open to new experiences can help you navigate these changes with grace and ease.

Your 50s is a time to harness the wisdom, experience and resilience you have built over the years. By focusing on health, maintaining strong and meaningful relationships, embracing lifelong learning and cultivating a positive mindset, you can be healthier and happier than ever before.

This is your time to shine and thrive.

Wishing You Joy, Health and Fulfilment.

Your Sister,

Keziah

Dear Married Couples,

REDISCOVERING LOVE AND CONNECTION IN YOUR MARRIAGE

Marriage is a journey that comes with its ups and downs. It is not uncommon for relationships to sometimes fall into a routine where love and genuine connection seem to be replaced by protocols and diplomacy. If you find yourselves in such a situation, it is essential to take proactive steps to rekindle the love and intimacy that initially brought you together. Here are some strategies to help you navigate this challenging phase:

Open Communication

1. **Honest Conversations:** Start with an open and honest conversation, conversations I term *"difficult yet necessary"* about how you both feel. Express your concerns and listen actively to your partner without interrupting or judging. Understanding each other's perspectives is the first step toward reconnection.

2. **Regular Check-ins:** Establish regular times to talk about your relationship – what I term, *"the state of the union"*. This could be a weekly or bi-weekly, monthly or quarterly *"relationship check-ins"* where you discuss what is going well and what needs improvement.

Rebuild Intimacy

1. **Quality Time:** Spend quality time together without distractions. This could mean regular date nights, weekend getaways or even simple activities like cooking a meal together, bathing together or taking a walk together.

2. **Physical Affection:** Physical touch is crucial in maintaining intimacy. Small gestures like holding hands, hugging or a gentle touch can go a long way in rebuilding a physical connection.

Seek Professional Help

1. **Couples Therapy:** A professional therapist can provide a safe space to explore underlying issues and help you develop strategies to improve your relationship.

3. **Workshops and Retreats:** Attend couples' workshops or retreats designed to strengthen relationships. These can provide valuable tools and new perspectives.

Focus on Positives

1. **Gratitude Practice:** Regularly express gratitude for your partner. Acknowledge and appreciate the positive aspects of your relationship and the qualities you love in your partner.

2. **Celebrate Small Wins:** Celebrate small achievements and milestones in your relationship. These moments of joy can help build a positive atmosphere.

Rediscover Shared Interests

1. **Common Hobbies:** Revisit activities you used to enjoy together or find new hobbies that you both find exciting. Shared interests can reignite the bond between you.

2. **Learn Together:** Taking up a new hobby or class together can create new memories and bring you closer. Working on your beliefs, paradigms and perspectives by roping your partner into your world is a big deal. You learn, unlearn and relearn together.

Personal Growth

1. **Self-Reflection:** Reflect on your own behaviour and attitudes. Consider what changes you can make to improve the relationship.

2. **Individual Fulfilment:** Ensure that you are also pursuing your individual passions and interests. A fulfilled person can contribute more positively to a relationship.

Reaffirm Commitment

1. **Revisit Vows:** Revisit and perhaps even renew your marriage vows. This can serve as a powerful reminder of your commitment to each other.

2. **Set Shared Goals:** Work together to set goals for your future. Having common objectives can strengthen your partnership and give you a sense of unity.

Marriage is an evolving partnership that requires effort, empathy and dedication from both sides. When love and connection seem to fade, taking conscious steps to rebuild and renew your relationship can make all the difference. By prioritizing communication, intimacy, shared activities and professional support, you can transform your marriage into a source of joy and fulfilment once again.

Wishing you both a journey of rediscovery and deepened love.

Best Regards,

Keziah

Dear Friends,

NAVIGATING LOVE, SEX AND DATING IN YOUR 50S: A GUIDE TO FULFILLING RELATIONSHIPS

I hope this letter finds you well and filled with the joy and wisdom that come with reaching your 50s. This stage of life brings new opportunities for self-discovery, growth and deepening relationships. In particular, love, sex and dating in your 50s can be a transformative and fulfilling journey. Allow me to share a guide that may help you embrace this chapter with confidence and create relationships that bring you joy and fulfilment.

Entering the 50s opens up a new chapter in your life, filled with opportunities for growth, joy and renewed connections. Whether you are single, divorced, widowed or simply looking to revitalize your current relationship, this period can be incredibly rewarding when it comes to love, sex and dating. Here are some insights and advice to help you navigate these aspects with confidence and excitement.

Embrace Self-Love and Confidence

1. **Self-Reflection:** Understand what you truly want in a relationship. Reflect on your experiences to identify what has worked well and what has not. This self-awareness can guide you toward healthier and more fulfilling relationships.

2. **Confidence Boost:** Embrace your age and the wisdom that comes with it. Confidence is attractive at any age. Feeling good about yourself is the first step in attracting a partner who appreciates you.

Reconnect with Your Partner

1. **Communication:** If you are in a long-term relationship, open lines of communication about your desires and needs. Honest conversations about sex, intimacy and emotional connection can reignite the spark.
2. **New Experiences:** Try new activities or hobbies together to create fresh memories and strengthen your bond. This can also include exploring new dimensions of your sexual relationship with mutual consent and openness.

Dating in Your 50s

1. **Online Dating:** Do not shy away from online dating platforms. Many are specifically designed for people in their 50s and beyond, offering a great way to meet like-minded individuals.
2. **Social Events:** Attend social events, join clubs and be active in groups that uphold your values or take classes that interest you.

These environments provide natural opportunities to meet new people and potentially find a romantic connection.

3. **Take It Slow:** There is no rush. Take the time to get to know someone before diving into a serious relationship. Enjoy the process of dating and learning about each other.

Navigating Sexual Health

1. **Health Check-ups:** Regular health check-ups are essential. Discuss any concerns with your doctor, including sexual health and function. They can provide advice and treatment if necessary.

2. **Communication and Consent:** Clear and open communication with your partner about sexual preferences and boundaries is crucial. Consent and mutual respect form the foundation of a healthy sexual relationship.

3. **Exploration:** Do not be afraid to explore new aspects of your sexuality. Whether it is trying new things in the bedroom or discussing fantasies with your partner, keeping an open mind can enhance your sexual satisfaction.

Building Emotional Intimacy

1. **Vulnerability:** Allow yourself to be vulnerable with your partner. Sharing your fears, hopes and dreams can deepen emotional intimacy and create a stronger connection.

2. **Quality Time:** Spend quality time together, free from distractions. This could mean regular date nights, weekend getaways or simply enjoying a quiet evening at home.

Rebuilding After Loss or Divorce

1. **Healing First:** If you have gone through a loss or divorce, give yourself time to heal before jumping into a new relationship. Grieving and processing emotions are important steps toward moving on healthily.

2. **Support System:** Lean on friends, family or support groups. Sharing your experiences and feelings with trustworthy and trusted people in your life who understand can be incredibly comforting

Your 50s can be a time of rediscovery and renewed passion in love, sex and dating. By embracing self-confidence, maintaining open communication, exploring new experiences and prioritizing your health, you can build fulfilling and joyful relationships. Remember, it is never too late to find love, reignite passion and enjoy meaningful connections.

Wishing you a journey filled with love and happiness.

Warm Regards,

Keziah

Dear Friends,

WHEN MARRIAGE BECOMES A GAME OF DIPLOMACY AND PROTOCOLS

I hope this letter finds you in good health and spirits. As we navigate through the different stages of life, relationships often evolve and change. It is common for marriages to become a game of diplomacy and protocols, where connection and communication may feel strained. I draw your attention with some advice to help you navigate this challenging situation and find renewed joy in your heart. Unlike my earlier letter to you, this scenario examines when you have tried everything possible yet there is no fulfilment in your heart concerning your marriage.

Some of you are married to spouses because of their social status, big men and big women in society; CEOs of companies, chiefs, leaders of religious groups, politicians, etc., awesome on profile yet your marriage life has become full of diplomacy and protocols, nothing to hold and to love.

The first category is those who married men for their potential and not their reality. That is *"the well to do man"*, financially solvent today although you married him when he had nothing to his name. You have struggled through life with him, built a life together, have children, properties, businesses yet there is no love, very apathetic.

Everyone sees him as generous and yet he is frugal with you. Some of you even stay in different houses, towns, cities or countries because of the nature of his work. The world sees you as married but all you have is his name – the title MRS. You have supported him so much that leaving the marriage seems like a loss to you so you are stuck.

The second category are those who married for true love. You have now come to terms that love is not enough to build any long-lasting relationship, you need commitment, accountability and growth, which he does not seem to have the capacity and mental fortitude to provide, yet you do not have the courage to walk away. Someone might ask why are you with a man who cannot lead you anywhere? Why are you with a man who for all these years has not put any plan in motion to own his life?

People forget that every woman marries with the hope that the man will evolve and be successful - his life will get better as the years go by so women will support with anticipation. What many women did not know at the point of marriage is that it will require the man to be ambitious enough to know where he wants to go with his life and how to get there. This will help him to create a space for his woman to be his helpmeet. A woman cannot drag her man up. Sometimes there is an attitudinal cooperation; the man has no idea of how to change his life even when the universe is awaiting his arising, his first step.

Your soul is bleeding now as a wife because, *"Hope deferred makes the heart sick, but a dream fulfilled is a tree of life."* **Proverbs 13:12**

The third category are the women who married for the prestige that comes with the man's status - the good and soft life. You thought money, material things and lavish lifestyle were enough. You now feel stuck, unhappy and unfulfilled.

Consider the following to keep you on the straight and narrow:

- Find comfort in your own company and understand self-sufficiency. Your socialization makes you think the man is to pay for everything financially. If he is a good man by your definition, but not ambitious in life, do not feel stagnated, you can work and get money to support your children, you chose a father for them, therefore improvise. As a woman, you are like a teabag; you have no idea how strong you are until you start living. Instead of being lonely, sad and depressed, be present in your children's lives if you have any. Money by itself cannot raise wholesome children. Motherhood has a penalty, my dear.

- Do not let marriage be your highest achievement in this life. Use your time to develop and deploy the woman in you. Go back to school, build a business, learn another language, pick a project and work on. Do something with your life that posterity will bless you for.

- Learn to compartmentalize your life.

  Your husband is to be your spouse and lover, that is if the marriage had marinated to lovers. The African woman has been socialized to see her husband as her father, brother, friend, lover, provider, protector, preserver, gossip partner - her everything, her god, right? No wonder unmet expectations are destroying relationships. You have a whole life to live; marriage is just an aspect of it, not its entirety.

- Know your psychology as a woman, understand yourself as a woman, you can do a swot analysis of your life.

SWOT analysis is a framework for identifying and analyzing an organization's strengths, weaknesses, opportunities and threats. The primary goal of SWOT analysis is to increase awareness of the factors that go into making a business decision or establishing a business strategy. Your life is a whole business and you are the CEO of it. List your needs from the important to the least important. Find out which of these your man can appropriately provide. If you are a single woman, learn. Choose a man that meets the most important ones for you so you can improvise for the rest.

Learn to build community around your other needs

- Seek professional help if your situation is affecting your mental health. Marriage is not oxygen; choose your peace of mind. Let your focus be on purpose.

- Take good care of yourself – spiritually, emotionally and financially. When you start taking good care of yourself, you will start to feel better, look better and emit better energy so you will receive better in return.

When a man who has paid your bride price decides to be audacious with disrespect, common sense tells you to be courageous with your boundaries. When a man starts treating you with contempt, know that his heart is no more with you. For your sanity and growth, learn to take a decision. You can cry in the storm or dance in the rain.

Some of you are stuck in these dysfunctional and unhealthy relationships because your lives are built all around these men. Without them, nothing is left of you. From your feeding, clothing to housing or accommodation – everything is on them. They know and therefore manipulate your lives to their tunes.

Are you a happy person? Do you want to live like this for the rest of your life?

When you hear people asking women to add value to our lives, all it simply means is to do something with our lives such that we will be able to support our lifestyles and our children should we run into such difficulties. In a part of the world where a man can decide not to cater for his biological children when the woman decides to walk away from unproductive relationship with him. Where it is normal for a father to use his responsibility for his children as a bait to get a woman stuck to him – these are indicators that mothers and women need to be financially solvent. Having children is a financial decision.

To the man who is equally stuck in a marriage with a testy and machiavellian wife - the opposite is equally true. The God who hates divorce equally hates dysfunctional marriage. Own your life and live for the sake of your sanity and growth.

Your Sister,

Keziah

Dear Friends,

BUILD THE FAMILY YOU DESIRE
BUILD COMMUNITY AROUND YOUR NEEDS

As we journey through our 50s, we often reflect on the importance of relationships and the support systems in our lives. Sometimes, our biological families may not provide the connection or support we need but this does not mean we have to face life's challenges alone. Creating a community around our needs and forming a chosen family can offer the companionship, support and fulfilment we all deserve.

Here are some steps and insights to help you build a meaningful and supportive community:

Recognize Your Needs

1. **Self-Assessment:** Take some time to understand what you need in terms of emotional support, companionship, practical help and social engagement. This self-awareness will guide you in identifying the right people to build your community.

2. **Define Your Values:** Consider what values are important to you in relationships, such as trust, mutual respect, kindness and shared interests. These values will help you attract like-minded individuals.

Expanding Your Social Circles

1. **Join Clubs and Groups:** Look for clubs, groups or classes that align with your interests and hobbies. Whether it is a book club, social media group, fitness class, prayer group, travel club or volunteer organization, these are great places to meet new people and build connections.

2. **Community Centres:** Many communities have centres that offer activities and social events for people in their 50s and older. Participate in these activities to meet new friends and potential support network members.

3. **Online Communities:** Do not underestimate the power of online communities. As Lisa Nichols, New York Times bestselling author and Motivational Speaker puts it *"It is not SOCIAL Media, it is Business Building Media, Contact Building Media, Credibility Building Media, Revenue Building Media, and Future Client Touching Media."* Join forums, social media groups or dating sites specifically for people in their 50s. These platforms can be valuable resources for building relationships and finding support.

Strengthening Existing Relationships

1. **Reconnect with Old Friends:** Reach out to old trusted and trustworthy friends or acquaintances with whom you have lost touch. Rekindling these relationships can bring a sense of continuity and shared history.

2. **Invest in Current Friendships:** Deepen your current friendships by spending more quality time together. Be open about your needs and encourage your friends to do the same.

Creating a Chosen Family

1. **Identify Key People:** Look for individuals who have been consistently supportive and trustworthy in your life. These could be friends, neighbours, colleagues or members of your community groups.
2. **Mutual Support:** Foster relationships based on mutual support. Offer your help and be there for others, creating a balanced dynamic where everyone feels valued and cared for.
3. **Shared Activities:** Engage in shared activities that strengthen your bond. This could include regular get-togethers, shared meals, travel or simply spending time together doing things you enjoy.

Building Emotional Intimacy

1. **Open Communication:** Be open and honest with your chosen family about your needs, feelings and expectations. Encourage them to do the same, creating a foundation of trust and understanding.
2. **Active Listening:** Practice active listening and empathy. Being genuinely present and attentive strengthens emotional connections.

Practical Support Systems

1. **Create Support Plans:** Develop plans on how you and your chosen family will support each other in practical and realistic ways.

2. **Emergency Contacts:** Make sure your chosen family members are aware of how to contact each other in case of emergencies. This ensures that someone will be there when you need help.

Building a supportive community and creating a chosen family in your 50s can bring immense joy, security and fulfilment. By understanding your needs, expanding your social circles and fostering deep, meaningful relationships, you can cultivate a network that enriches your life and provides the support you deserve. Remember, family is not just about blood relations; it is about the connections we make and the love we share.

Here is to building a community that truly serves and uplifts you. With warm regards and best wishes for your journey.

Your Sister,

Keziah

Dear Friends,

COUNT YOUR BLESSINGS NOT YOUR BURDENS

As we journey through our 50s, it is natural to reflect on our lives, assessing our achievements and the challenges we have faced. This period often brings a mixture of emotions but it also offers a unique opportunity to shift our perspective towards gratitude and anticipation for the future. By focusing on our blessings rather than our burdens, we can cultivate a more positive outlook and a greater sense of excitement for the years ahead. Embrace gratitude and look forward to an exciting future.

Count Your Blessings

1. **Reflect on Achievements:** Take time to acknowledge and celebrate your accomplishments, both big and small. Reflecting on your successes can boost your self-esteem and remind you of your resilience and capabilities. If not for anything; for the gift of life. You can march on because you are alive.

2. **Appreciate Relationships:** Cherish the relationships that have enriched your life - family, friends, colleagues and community. These connections provide support, love and joy. They are also a testament to the meaningful bonds you have built.

3. **Health and Wellness:** Recognize and be grateful for your health and the ability to pursue activities you enjoy. If you have overcome health challenges, acknowledge the strength and determination it took to do so.

4. **Life Experiences:** Appreciate the diverse experiences that have shaped you. Whether they were joyous or challenging, each experience has contributed to your growth and wisdom.

Shift Focus from Burdens

1. **Practice Mindfulness:** Mindfulness techniques such as meditation and deep breathing can help you stay present and focused on the positive aspects of your life. These practices can reduce stress and shift your mindset from worry to gratitude.

2. **Positive Affirmations:** Incorporate positive affirmations into your daily routine. Remind yourself of your strengths, your worth and the good things in your life. This simple practice can significantly improve your outlook. The I am statements are powerful. "I am a powerful daughter of a powerful universe, the infinite power." What do you say to yourself?

3. **Let Go of Negativity:** Identify and release negative thoughts or grievances that may be weighing you down. Holding on to negativity can prevent you from fully appreciating the present and looking forward to the future.

Embrace the Future with Excitement

1. **Set New Goals:** Setting new, inspiring goals can create a sense of purpose and excitement.

   Whether it is learning a new skill, traveling, volunteering or starting a new business, having something to look forward to can invigorate your spirit.

2. **Explore Opportunities:** Your 50s is a great time to explore new opportunities and experiences. Be open to trying new things, meeting new people, and stepping out of your comfort zone.

3. **Invest in Yourself:** Focus on self-care and personal development. This might include pursuing further education, engaging in physical fitness or indulging in activities that bring you joy and fulfilment.

Cultivate Gratitude

1. **Gratitude Journal:** Keep a gratitude journal to record daily blessings and positive experiences. Reflecting on these entries regularly can reinforce a grateful mindset and highlight the abundance in your life.

2. **Express Gratitude:** Take the time to express gratitude to those around you. A simple thank you, a heartfelt note or a kind gesture can strengthen relationships and spread positivity.

3. **Celebrate Milestones:** Celebrate personal milestones and achievements, no matter how small. Acknowledging these moments fosters a sense of accomplishment and joy.

Your 50s can be a time of renewed enthusiasm, purpose and joy. By focusing on your blessings rather than your burdens and embracing the future with excitement, you can create a fulfilling and vibrant life. Remember, gratitude is a powerful tool that can transform your outlook and open your heart to new possibilities. I do not know about you but I am super excited about the future - greater and fulfilling rewards for all our labour this time around.

Here is to appreciating the present and eagerly anticipating the future. With Warm Regards and Best Wishes,

Keziah

Dear Friends,

WHAT LEGACY ARE YOU LEAVING FOR THE NEXT GENERATION?

As we navigate through our 50s, it is a pivotal time to reflect not only on our own lives but also on the legacy we are creating for future generations. We have the power to change the trajectory of our lineage by setting a positive example and laying a strong foundation for prosperous living. This letter is to inspire and guide you in becoming a beacon of hope and prosperity for your family and the generations to follow. Pave the way for a prosperous future for generations to come.

Embrace Lifelong Learning

1. **Continued Education:** Commit to lifelong learning. Whether through formal education, online courses, or self-study, expanding your knowledge can inspire younger generations to value education and personal growth. Let your children and grandchildren see and know that you are personally and intellectually improving. You do not need to go back to school if you do not want. Learning has become very easy today. We can learn from multiple sources apart from going to school. There are many things we can learn to improve our lives and be the role models for our generation that no educational content can teach.

2. **Skills Development:** Sharpen existing skills or acquire new ones.This not only enhances your own life but also demonstrates the importance of adaptability and continuous improvement.

Financial Wisdom

1. **Financial Literacy:** Educate yourself and your family about financial management. Understanding budgeting, savings, investing and responsible spending sets a strong example for financial stability.

2. **Estate Planning:** Ensure your estate planning is in order. Wills, trusts and clear instructions can prevent future conflicts and ensure your assets are passed down according to your wishes.

3. **Generational Wealth:** Think long-term about how to create and sustain generational wealth. This might involve investing in education funds for grandchildren or teaching family members about smart investments.

Health and Wellness

1. **Healthy Lifestyle:** Lead by example in maintaining a healthy lifestyle. Regular exercise, a balanced diet and mental health care are crucial. Encourage family members to adopt these habits for their long-term well-being.

2. **Preventive Care:** Prioritize regular medical check-ups and preventive care. Show that proactive health management can lead to a longer and healthier life.

Strong Family Bonds

1. **Quality Time:** Invest in spending quality time with your family. Shared experiences and memories strengthen bonds and create a supportive family environment.

2. **Open Communication:** Foster an environment of open communication. Encourage family members to express their thoughts and feelings, which can help resolve conflicts and build stronger relationships.

3. **Traditions and Values:** Pass down family traditions and values. Whether through storytelling, family rituals or shared activities, these practices can instil a sense of identity and continuity.

Leading by Example

1. **Integrity and Ethics:** Live with integrity and strong ethical values. Your actions and decisions set a powerful example for younger generations about the importance of honesty, responsibility and fairness.

2. **Resilience and Perseverance:** Demonstrate resilience in the face of challenges. Show that perseverance and a positive attitude can overcome obstacles and inspire others to do the same.

3. **Community Involvement:** Get involved in community service and charitable activities. By contributing to the greater good, you highlight the importance of compassion, empathy and social responsibility.

Encouraging Ambition and Dreams

1. **Support Aspirations:** Encourage your family members to pursue their dreams and aspirations. Provide support, whether emotional, financial or educational to help them achieve their goals.
2. **Mentorship:** Act as a mentor to younger family members. Share your experiences, offer guidance and provide a listening ear to help them navigate their own journeys.

Changing the trajectory of your lineage and setting a prosperous example for future generations is a noble and impactful endeavour. By focusing on lifelong learning, financial wisdom, a healthy lifestyle, strong family bonds, ethical living and community involvement, you can create a legacy of prosperity and resilience.

Remember, the actions you take today can shape the future for those who follow, making your 50s a powerful time to influence and inspire. Even if you were born into a poor home, do not die poor. Set a bar for your lineage to aspire to.

Here is to a legacy of prosperity and positive impact for generations to come.

With Warm Regards and Best Wishes,

Keziah

Dear Friends,

EMBRACE YOUR PURPOSE AND SELF-ACTUALIZATION IN YOUR 50S

As we enter our 50s, it is an ideal time to reflect on our lives, values and the path we want to forge ahead. This stage of life offers a wonderful opportunity to focus on what truly matters: finding purpose and self-actualization rather than chasing popularity or falling into the trap of people pleasing. Here is some advice to help you embark on this enriching journey.

Discover Your Purpose

1. **Reflect on Your Passions:** Think about what activities or causes ignite your passion. What have you always enjoyed or felt deeply about? Reflecting on these can help you identify your true purpose.
2. **Set Meaningful Goals:** Establish goals that align with your values and passions. These goals should inspire and challenge you, offering a sense of accomplishment and fulfilment as you work toward them.
3. **Give Back:** Consider how you can contribute to your community or causes you care about. Volunteering, mentoring or engaging in charitable activities can provide a profound

sense of purpose. What questions can you answer? What needs can you satisfy?

Focus on Self-Actualization

1. **Continuous Learning:** Embrace lifelong learning. Whether it is through formal education, workshops, reading or exploring new hobbies, continuously expanding your knowledge and skills can lead to personal growth and self-fulfilment.

2. **Mindfulness and Self-Reflection:** Practice mindfulness and self-reflection regularly. These practices can help you stay grounded, understand your true self and navigate life's challenges with clarity and calm.

3. **Creative Expression:** Engage in creative activities that allow you to express yourself. This could be the art of speaking, music, writing or any other form of creativity that brings you joy and satisfaction.

Avoid People-Pleasing

1. **Set Boundaries:** Learn to set healthy boundaries. It is important to recognize your limits and communicate them clearly to others. This ensures you are respecting your own needs and not overextending yourself to please others.

2. **Authenticity over Approval:** Focus on being authentic rather than seeking approval. Being true to yourself and your values will attract genuine relationships and lead to greater self-respect and happiness.

3. **Say No When Needed:** Do not be afraid to say no. It is okay to prioritize your well-being and commitments over trying to meet everyone else's expectations.

Embrace Meaningful Relationships

1. **Quality Over Quantity:** Seek quality relationships that are based on mutual respect, understanding and shared values. These relationships are more fulfilling and supportive than a large circle of acquaintances.

2. **Open Communication:** Foster open and honest communication in your relationships. Being able to express your true feelings and listen to others can deepen your connections and provide emotional support.

3. **Surround Yourself with Positivity:** Surround yourself with people who uplift and inspire you. Positive relationships can significantly influence your journey toward self-actualization and purpose.

Prioritize Self-Care

1. **Physical Health:** Take good care of your physical health through regular exercise, a balanced diet and adequate rest.

A healthy body supports a healthy mind and enhances your ability to pursue your purpose.

2. **Mental Well-Being:** Pay attention to your mental health. Engage in activities that reduce stress, such as meditation, deep breathing or spending time in nature. Seek professional help if needed.

3. **Emotional Balance:** Practice self-compassion and emotional resilience. Accept and understand your emotions and work on building a positive mindset.

Your 50s is a time of immense potential for personal growth, fulfilment and self-actualization. By focusing on what truly matters, setting meaningful goals, embracing authenticity and nurturing positive relationships, you can lead a purposeful and satisfying life. Remember, the journey to self-fulfilment is unique to each individual and it is never too late to start living a life that resonates with your true self. No one can go back and make a brand new start; however, anyone can start from now and make a brand new ending.

Wishing you a journey filled with purpose and joy.

Much Love and Blessings,

Keziah

BIBLIOGRAPHY

1. Betterhelp Editorial Team, April 16, 2024:
   https://www.betterhelp.com/advice/personality-disorders/the-psychology-behind-sense-of-entitlement/

2. Sandra Dalton-Smith, MD 6th January 2021:
   https://ideas.ted.com/the-7-types-of-rest-that-every-person-needs/

3. Dr. Debi Silber: Founder and CEO of The PBT (Post Betrayal Transformation) Institute
   https://thepbtinstitute.com/7-physical-dangers-of-resentment-and-bitterness

Another book by Keziah Twumasi

ABOUT ZIZIKARL FOUNDATION

The story of Zizikarl Foundation is a remarkable one of faith, hope and love. It is a story of a woman who understood the revelation that you can invest lessons from your pain into someone else's life in order to ease their pain. Keziah Twumasi, the woman in question took a firm decision to do just that.

Our three focus areas are:

- Marriage and Family Life
- Women and Youth in development
- Educational / Vocational training

Our vision is to:

- Guide young adults to reconnect with themselves, own their lives and live their dreams.

- Enlighten would-be couples to pursue a purpose-driven relationship

- Empower married couples to understand their challenges and priorities, and guide them through their choices irrespective of their religious backgrounds.

Our objectives are:

- Leading young adults to identify their gifts and talents to develop and deploy them.
- Teaching singles to live fulfilled lives.
- Creating the opportunity for shared experiences to inform behavioural change in family life.
- Helping couples as well as individuals to identify challenges, priorities and areas of change in their lives.

We provide counselling that equips singles, courting and married couples to find practical, realistic and sustainable solutions to the challenges in their relationships and set the pace for in-depth dialogue that leads to personal fulfilment as well as development of close relationships.

Contact Us: Zizikarl Foundation, P. O. Box AK 320, Akosombo

+233 (0) 343021895 or +233 (0) 244153861

Facebook: keziahtwumasi

Instagram: Keziah.twumasi

Youtube: Keziah twumasi

Twitter: KeziahTwumasi

Clubhouse: keziahtwumasi